vegetarian sushi

THE ESSENTIAL KITCHEN

vegetarian sushi

BRIGID TRELOAR

PERIPLUS

contents

vegetarian sushi

Sushi, and in particular, vegetarian sushi, is not just a delicious food but an edible work of art. When beautifully prepared and elegantly presented, sushi is a balanced composition of flavor, texture and color that is a feast for the eyes and a treat for the palate. Using only the freshest ingredients and subtle seasonings, sushi is tasty, healthy, convenient to eat and satisfying without being overpowering.

One of the world's first "fast foods," sushi has long been a part of Japanese culture. Vegetarianism also has a long history in Japan, especially as a temple food for monks.

However, although the exact origin of sushi is unclear, it is commonly accepted that it is based on an ancient Asian practice of preserving fish in salt and rice, first introduced to Japan from Southeast Asia and China in the seventh century AD. Originally, the rice was discarded, but over time when vinegar was added to quicken the fermentation process, it was discovered that the fermented rice was also delicious.

Over the years, regional differences developed in Japanese cuisine. A range of seafood, vegetables and soybean products were added to the basic rice to form a variety of creative sushi combinations, and all are excellent nutritionally.

A common misconception is that sushi and sashimi are the same. They are not. Sushi always includes seasoned rice, while sashimi, which means "raw" in Japanese, is raw, fresh seafood. Although sushi may include some raw fish, many other ingredients are also used, such as fresh, seasoned and pickled vegetables, seasoned omelette and tofu. Sushi is a balanced food. As with other Japanese dishes, sushi contains five basic tastes, all essential for good taste and good health: sour from the vinegar in sushi rice, bitter and salt from the soy sauce, hot from the wasabi and sweet from the rice. It is believed that slight bitterness and hotness are essential to harmonize and balance the entire taste of a dish.

Modern influences and ingredients from outside of Japan have stimulated flexibility and creativity in sushi making. There is an annual Sushi Day competition in Japan where the most intricate patterns and edible pictures are created that are a sight to behold.

Some sushi require great skill to make. In Japan, sushi chefs are trained and their talents highly regarded, but some sushi is deceptively simple even for the novice to make. Whether sushi is small bite-sized balls of seasoned rice with a variety of toppings (nigiri-zushi), large or small sushi rolls (maki-zushi), sushi in a box or bowl (chirashi-zushi) or even sushi that guests can make themselves (temaki-zushi), all sushi has one thing in common: It should always look as good as it tastes.

Serving sushi

Sushi is made with the fingers and can be eaten with the fingers or chopsticks.

Present artful arrangements of sushi on a platter or individual dishes with gari (pickled ginger slices) and wasabi (Japanese horseradish) on the side. Gari is eaten between different types of sushi to cleanse the palate. Fiery wasabi is used in many sushi and also added to sushi by diners according to taste. Also provide individual bowls of Japanese

soy sauce for dipping. Japanese soy sauce is slightly sweeter than other soy sauce and better compliments the food, whereas others are often too salty, too strong and overpower the delicate flavors. Contrary to popular belief, wasabi should not be mixed into the soy sauce when eating sushi, as it dilutes two flavors. Place a small amount of wasabi on the sushi with a finger or chopstick, then dip into the sauce.

Sushi can be served alone as an appetizer or light meal or as a course in a larger meal. A simple yet complete sushi meal combines sushi with miso or suimono (clear) soup and pickles with fresh fruit for dessert and, of course, green tea.

Serve suimono, which means "something to drink," as a first course or part-way through a meal as a palate refresher. Simple, natural and fresh, it should not dull the appetite but stimulate the taste buds to appreciate all the delicate flavors. It should be impressive in its purity and restraint. The heartier miso soup can be a meal in itself, and should be served with or after the sushi. If possible, serve Japanese soups, both thick and thin, in covered lacquer bowls, which keep the soup hot but allow the bowl to stay cool enough to be picked up.

Japanese desserts are very simple, if served at all. Fresh fruit, decoratively cut and beautifully presented, provides an elegant finish to a sushi meal. Today, green tea ice cream is often served to cleanse and refresh the palate.

Hot green tea is considered essential to the full enjoyment of sushi as it also cleanses the palate and refreshes the mouth, removing any aftertaste between bites. The thick tea cups used for Japanese tea are left-over from the days of outdoor stalls, where water was often in short supply and busy proprietors found it more efficient to pour green tea into a large, heat-retaining cup so it had to be topped up less often.

Traditionally, an unlimited supply of green tea is served throughout the meal. Beer, sake and more recently, white wine, have become popular also. Sake, like wine, can be either sweet or dry, and may be drunk chilled or warm. The choice is a matter of personal taste, and although sake has always been considered a must in Japan, there are divided opinions about serving it with sushi, as both are made from rice.

Using vegetarian ingredients in sushi

Sushi making is limited only by your imagination. While traditionally, sushi is largely based on seafood, rice and vegetables, vegetarian sushi uses a much larger variety of fresh, seasoned and pickled vegetables that allows sushi lovers to make the most of seasonal produce. One of the most important things this book shows you is how to experiment with different combinations of vegetables to create wonderfully colorful and flavorful sushi.

Look for commercial pickled vegetables in Asian markets and larger supermarkets or make your own. Always use the best quality and freshest produce available. Buy quality vegetables in season when they are less expensive and pickle them for later use.

Flavor, color and texture

When creating any type of sushi, keep in mind not only flavor but also color and texture. Retaining the individual taste and appearance of each ingredient is very important to making the most of fresh, natural and seasonal foods. No individual flavor should be overpowering or too strong. Utilize ingredients such as Japanese soy sauce whenever possible, as they are specifically suited to the more delicate flavors of Japanese food.

Benefits of including sushi in a vegetarian diet

Sushi, an exquisite food, is also one of the healthiest and most nutritional foods available. Rice, vegetables, soy and nori are basic vegetarian sushi ingredients, all readily available and all excellent nutritionally. Rice is high in carbohydrates, vegetables contain no fat (with the exception of avocado which contains good fat) and are rich in fiber and contain essential vitamins, minerals and phytochemicals, which help to protect the body from disease. Ginger and Japanese pickles in particular, aid digestion and help fight colds and flu. Nori (seaweed) is also a rich source of vitamins and minerals, particularly iodine, which aids in the prevention of cholesterol build-up in the blood vessels.

Soy beans in the form of tofu, soy sauce, miso and natto also provide high protein, magnesium, potassium and iron, with phytoestrogens and isoflavens being used to fight menopause problems, lower cholesterol, reduce heart disease, aid in the prevention of cancer (breast and prostate) and osteoperosis. Miso based soups, which are so easy and quick to prepare, can provide about one sixth of the daily adult requirement of protein. Based on any type of miso, from salty to sweet, and served with other ingredients and seasonings, it can be a nutritious meal in itself.

Rice is also a good source of dietary fiber. Brown rice has long been considered in many Asian countries suitable only

for the poorer, lower class people who could not afford the more processed, polished white rice. But recent research shows that any rice is high in resistant starch, which is beneficial for a healthy bowel and makes you feel full, which lessens the tendency to snack between meals.

There are two other very important factors that add to the nutritional benefits of eating sushi. It is a well-known dieting procedure that chewing your food well aids in digestion and makes you feel less hungry. Sushi rice is fairly firm and therefore requires chewing longer. This allows the appetite nerve center of the brain to receive the signals of satiety, and hence aid in eating less!

Remember, one of the healthy ways of eating food is in a pleasant atmosphere. Whether in a sushi bar, with the chatter of the sushi chef and customers, or at home, the practice of sharing balanced and beautiful food makes for a wonderful and healthy experience.

Suggested serving sizes

Sushi type	Fillings	Nori	Sushi rice (cooked)
Large sushi roll (Futomaki-zushi)	5–6	1 sheet	1 cup
Small sushi roll (Hosomaki-zushi)	1–2	½ sheet	½ cup
Inside-out sushi roll (Uramaki-zushi)	3–4	½ sheet	¾ cup
Topping on rice ball (Nigiri-zushi)	1 slice or topping		1½ tablespoons (6–7 per cup)
Seasoned tofu pouches (Inari-zushi)			2 tablespoons (5 per cup)
Hand-wrapped sushi (Temaki-zushi)	2–4	¼ or ½	1½ tablespoons (6–7 per cup)
Battleship sushi (Gunkan maki-zushi)	1 topping	1 strip, 1 inch by 5 inches (2 cm by 13 cm)	1½ tablespoons (2 teaspoons for mini size)

Mixed plate

4 Nigiri-zushi
1 small roll (hosomaki-zushi) (6 pieces)
2 battleship sushi (gunkan maki-zushi)
1 seasoned tofu pouch (inari-zushi)
OR
1 small roll (hosomaki-zushi) (6 pieces)
½ large sushi roll (futomaki-zushi) (4 pieces)
2 seasoned tofu pouches (inari-zushi)

Type of Sushi		Sushi for 2	Sushi for 4	Sushi for 6-8
(1 cup prepared sushi rice = 150 g)				
Large sushi roll	No. rolls (8 pieces)	2 (16 pieces)	4 (32 pieces)	6–8 (48–64 pieces)
(Futomaki-zushi)	Sushi rice (cups)	2	4	6–8
	Nori sheets	2	4	6–8
	Fillings	2 x 5–6	4 x 5–6	6–8 x 5–6
Small sushi roll	No. rolls (6 pieces)	4 (24 pieces)	8 (48 pieces)	12–16 (72–96 pieces)
(Hosomaki-zushi)	Sushi rice (cups)	2	4	6–8
	Nori sheets	2	4	6–8
	No. fillings	4 x 1–2	8 x 1–2	12–16 x 1–2
Inside-out sushi roll	No. rolls (8 pieces)	3	6	9–12
(Uramaki-zushi)	Sushi rice (cups)	2¼	4½	7–9
	Nori sheets	1½	3	4½–6
	No. fillings	3 x 4–5	6 x 4–5	9–12 x 4–5
Nigiri-zushi	No.	20	40	60–80
(topping on rice ball)	Sushi rice	3 cups	6 cups	9–12 cups
	Toppings	20	40	60–80
Seasoned tofu pouches	No. pouches	6	12	18–24
(Inari-zushi)	Sushi rice	12 tablespoons	24 tablespoons	36–48 tablespoons
	2 tablespoons per pouch (5 per cup)	(1¼ cups)	(2½ cups)	(4–5 cups)
	Ties (seasoned kampyo)	6	12	18–24
Hand-wrapped sushi	No.	18	36	54–72
(Temaki-zushi)	Sushi rice	3 cups	5½ cups	8–11 cups
	No. fillings	18 x 2–4	36 x 2–4	45–72 x 2–4
Battleship sushi	No.	6	12	18–24
(Gunkan maki-zushi)	Sushi rice	1 cup	2 cups	3–3¾ cups

ingredients

Pickled vegetables

Beni-shoga: Pickled red ginger made with older season ginger. More savory than the pink variety (gari). Available sliced or shredded in packets or jars.

Gari: Pickled pink ginger made with early season ginger. Sweeter than the red variety (beni-shoga). Available sliced in packets and jars.

Kimchee: Korean spicy fermented cabbage. Kimchee is strongly flavored, so use only a small quantity. Although not traditionally Japanese, kimchee has become popular as an accompaniment to sushi and other Japanese dishes.

Pickled eggplant: Serve as a side dish with sushi or in sushi rolls.

Takuan: Pickled daikon radish that is colored yellow. Some are flavored with seaweed or chili. Sold whole or sliced in vacuum sealed packs. Keeps well refrigerated after opening. Use in sushi rolls or as a side dish of pickles.

Umeboshi plums, pitted or Umeboshi paste: Salty pickled plums. These are available whole and in paste form. Keep opened packets in the refrigerator.

Fresh or seasoned ingredients

Bamboo shoots: Tender but crispy shoots, available in cans from most stores. Used for texture rather than flavor.

Bonito flakes: These large sandy brown flakes of smoked and dried bonito fish are used to make dashi, which is a basic Japanese stock. The small flakes, sold in small cellophane packets, are used as a garnish.

Cellophane noodles: Also known as bean thread or harusame noodles. Gossamer, translucent threads are made from the starch of green mung beans, potato starch or sweet potato starch. They are sold dried and so must be soaked in hot water to soften before using.

Cilantro: Also known as coriander or Chinese parsley. Available fresh, the roots, stems and leaves are all used in cooking. The leaves are used for garnishing and are strongly flavored, so use sparingly.

Cucumber: English (hothouse), telegraph (long) and Lebanese variety are all suitable. Cucumber should be seeded so that sushi does not become too moist (leave skin on). Cut cucumber lengthwise into quarters or thinly slice.

Daikon: Long white radish with a slightly hot flavor.

Dashi: This traditional Japanese stock, which is made from bonito fish flakes (katsuobushi) and konbu (seaweed), is the basis of many Japanese dishes. Granules or liquid instant dashi is readily available. If a completely vegetarian stock is required, use only konbu and double the quantity.

Dried somen noodles: Thin, white noodles made from wheat flour.

Fu: Wheat gluten in small decorative shapes. Sold dried.

Ginger: The thick, rootlike rhizome of the ginger plant has a sharp, pungent flavor. Ginger should be firm, with a smooth skin. Once the thin, tan skin is peeled away from fresh ginger, with the back of a knife, the flesh is sliced or grated. Store fresh ginger in the refrigerator. See also gari and beni-shoga.

Glace ginger: Sweet candied ginger.

Kampyo: Dried strips of gourd used as a decorative tie around foods. Must be rubbed in salt and water to soften and cooked before use. See also Kampyo, seasoned.

Kampyo, seasoned: Strips of gourd simmered in sweetened soy sauce (see page 24). Available in cans and refrigerated packets.

Konbu: Also kombu. Dried giant kelp or seaweed. Basis of Japanese stock. Washing before use results in lost flavor. Cut edges or cut into pieces to release extra flavor. Should be removed from stock before boiling or taste becomes bitter.

Lotus root (renkon): If using fresh, peel, slice and leave in lightly vinegared water until required. Otherwise use frozen or dried lotus root or pickled lotus in packets.

Miso: Fermented soy bean paste. Many varieties are available, including red, white, salt-reduced, and some mixed with other cereals (eg. rice). General rule is the darker the color the saltier the taste. Light and dark can be mixed for interesting flavors.

Mushrooms, enoki: Clumps of tiny white mushroom heads on long, thin stalks. Use in soups and in nabemono dishes (one pot dishes).

Mushrooms, shiitake: Available fresh or dried. Dried mushrooms have a more concentrated flavor so use sparingly. Soften dried shiitake in lukewarm water for 30 minutes. Discard stems, as they do not soften.

PICKLED VEGETABLES

FRESH & SEASONED INGREDIENTS

Mushrooms, shimeji: Clusters of straw-colored mushrooms with small heads. Use in soups and nabemono (one pot dishes).

Natto: Fermented soybeans with a rich flavor, similar to cheese, a pungent odor and a rather glutinous consistency. Many Japanese enjoy natto for breakfast over hot rice, but it is also used in miso soup.

Red miso paste: See Miso.

Seasoned tofu: See under wrappers.

Sesame seeds: Black and white are available raw and toasted from Asian food stores. Toast sesame seeds in a dry frying pan over medium heat, shaking pan constantly to prevent burning. When seeds begin to brown and pop remove from heat. For sesame paste, grind hot seeds until smooth or use tahini. Toasting brings out the flavor.

Shiso: Mild-flavored Japanese herb that is a member of the mint family. Often available fresh. Use in sushi rolls (see recipe page 46 and variation page 42) or as a garnish. Keep airtight and refrigerated. Red leaves are used mainly to color pickles.

Soba noodles: Noodles made from buckwheat flour, wheat flour and sometimes powdered green tea.

Sushi rice: Short or medium grain rice that just clings together without being clumpy when cooked. Koshihikari is short grain, Calrose is a medium rice. Note: Sushi rice is not sticky rice, which is a glutinous rice mainly used for sweets.

Tahini: Thick paste made of ground sesame seeds. Substitute for toasted white sesame seeds.

Toasted pine nuts: Toast pine nuts in a dry frying pan over medium heat, until golden brown, shaking pan constantly to prevent burning. Toasting brings out flavor.

Toasted sesame seeds (white and black): See sesame seeds.

Tofu: Soybean curd, available fresh or long-life, soft or firm, sold in blocks. Keep refrigerated, covered with water, which should be changed daily (use within 5 days). Tofu will readily absorb the flavors it's cooked or marinated in. Tofu retains liquid and should be well drained before use. To drain, place block of tofu on a chopping board at 45 degrees. Place another chopping board or plate with a weight on top, and let stand for 30 minutes. Tofu can also be boiled for a few minutes before use to expel excess liquid and make tofu firmer or grilled until lightly browned on both sides for firmer texture and nutty flavor. Grilled tofu is also available in cans.

Wakame: A type of seaweed available in dried form that is reconstituted in water and becomes bright green. Wakame is used in soups, salads, simmered dishes, and is finely chopped through rice.

White miso paste: See Miso.

Seasonings and condiments

Aka oroshi: Japanese red chili paste. This is mixed with grated daikon radish and used as a garnish for white-fish sushi. Do not substitute other types of chili paste, as they will probably be too pungent. Alternatively, push a few dried red chilies into a piece of daikon and grate finely or sprinkle chili flakes over grated daikon.

Asian sesame oil: Has a darker, stronger flavor and fragrance than the lighter one. Used as a flavor accent.

Chili peppers: As a general rule, the smaller the chili the hotter the flavor regardless of the color. Remove seeds and membranes to reduce heat.

Chili sauce or sweet chili sauce: Although not traditional, this spicy blend of tomatoes, chilies and onions can be used as a dipping sauce in or with sushi.

Chives and garlic chives: Fragrant herb with thin green stems and mild onion (chives) or onion and garlic (garlic chives) flavor. Use fresh in sushi rolls or as a decorative tie.

Ichimi togarashi: Ground chili powder used as a seasoning (see also shichimi togarashi).

Konbu: Also known as kombu. Dried kelp. This sea vegetable is available in the form of hard, flat black sheets that often have a fine white powder on the surface. Konbu is used to flavor dashi, a basic soup stock, and sushi rice. Wipe the surface of the sheets with a damp cloth before use. Do not wash the konbu as you will diminish its flavor. Avoid konbu that is wrinkled and thin.

Lemon zest: Use a lemon zester to thinly shred and curl lemon peel, or grate finely.

Mayonnaise: Japanese mayonnaise is creamy and less sweet than western mayonnaise. For more bite add wasabi to make wasabi mayonnaise.

Mirin: Sweet rice wine for cooking. Can substitute sweet sherry.

Sake: Japanese fermented rice wine. Sake is used in cooking to tenderize meat and fish, and to make ingredients more flavorful. It also counteracts acidity. Buy cooking sake (ryoriyo sake) or inexpensive drinking sake for making sushi.

Shichimi togarashi: Seven spice mix, based on hot peppers. Used as a seasoning.

Soy sauce, Japanese: Slightly sweeter than other soy. Enhances but does not drown delicate flavors. Do not use other Asian soy sauces as the flavor is too strong and often too salty.

WRAPPERS

SEASONINGS & CONDIMENTS

Sushi vinegar: Mixture of rice vinegar, sugar and salt (see page 28). Available prepared in liquid or powder form. There are different styles and flavors of sushi vinegar in Japan—some sweet, some salty. The proportions of the three ingredients, rice vinegar, sugar and salt, can be varied according to personal taste. Commercial sushi vinegar can be purchased at most Asian grocery stores and even some larger western supermarkets. Sushi vinegar can be made ahead and refrigerated in an airtight container. If making your own, make sure sugar and salt have dissolved before use.

Teriyaki sauce: Made from soy sauce, mirin, sake and sugar. Available from Asian food stores and larger western supermarkets, or try the recipe on page 105.

Wasabi: Very hot Japanese green horseradish. Used sparingly to enhance flavors. Refrigerate paste after opening, or mix powder with water to required consistency. Prepare wasabi just before required and keep covered as it loses flavor quickly. Some chefs keep it in a bowl upside down, a good way to check if consistency is correct. Fresh wasabi is sometimes available. Peel with the back of a knife and grate in a circular motion on a very fine grater only as required. Inexpensive graters made especially for this are readily available from Asian markets.

Sushi wrappers

Abura-age: thinly sliced, deep-fried tofu. Pour boiling water over tofu or simmer in boiling water for 1–2 minutes and gently squeeze to remove excess oil and water before use. See Seasoned tofu.

Belgian endive (witloof): slightly bitter tasting leaves. Can be filled with sushi rice.

Blanched cabbage leaves: Rinse leaves to remove dirt and mirowave 1–2 minutes, or simmer in boiling water until leaves just softened, 1–2 minutes. Immediately rinse under cold water to stop the cooking process.

Blanched spinach leaves: Rinse leaves to remove dirt and mirowave 1–2 minutes, or simmer in boiling water until leaves just softened, 1–2 minutes. Immediately rinse under cold water to stop the cooking process and set color.

Lettuce leaves, raw or blanched: if using to wrap sushi rolls drop leaves into boiling water, or microwave for 1–2 minutes to soften. Immediately rinse under cold water to stop the cooking process.

Nori: Toasted seaweed (yaki-nori) used as a wrapper for sushi rolls (see page 32). Usually sold in packs of 10. Keep airtight. Can be refrigerated for 1 month or frozen for 3–4 months once opened. Although they can still be used after this time, optimum color and flavor may be lost. Pass one side only over a moderate gas flame or place under the griller for a few seconds before use if untoasted or if toasted seaweed needs to be freshened and crisped. It is better to buy yaki-nori in smaller quantities more often.

Seasoned tofu (seasoned abura-age): thinly sliced, deep-fried tofu that has been simmered in sweetened soy sauce (see page 64). One side is cut so tofu can be opened to form a pouch which can be stuffed with sushi rice (see page 66). Seasoned tofu pouches are available in packets or canned from Asian food stores.

Thin seasoned omelette (usuyaki tamago): Thin omelette used as a wrapper for sushi rolls (see pages 26 and 88), sushi pouches (see page 86) or sushi cones (see page 88).

Yuba (soymilk skin): this is the skin formed when soymilk is heated. It is highly nutritious and is available in dried or frozen sheets. Soak each sheet in warm water for 30 seconds to soften, then pat dry with paper towel before use.

Cucumber curls: Thinly peel around the cucumber at 45 degrees. Reshape into a cone and fill with condiments (such as wasabi) to use as a garnish on a sushi platter.

Cucumber decoration: Slice an unpeeled cucumber about ¼ inch (6 mm) thick 2½ inches (6 cm) long and ¾ inch (2 cm) wide. Cut into an odd number of thin strips leaving ¾ inch (2 cm) uncut at one end. Fold every second strip down towards the middle.

Cucumber or radish cups: Slice the base off a fresh red radish or cut a piece of unpeeled cucumber about 1¼ inches (3 cm) long. Make three or four 45 degree cuts downwards around the radish or cucumber and discard the middle section. Use the decorative cup as a dish for condiments, such as wasabi or mustard. Soak radish cup in ice water to open the petals more. Fill with contrasting condiment color for best decoration.

Decorative leaves: Lay fresh, washed, pesticide free camellia or lemon leaves flat and cut "D" section out from either side of central vein with a sharp knife or scalpel.

Ginger rose: Lay pieces of pickled ginger across a chopping board, each one slightly overlapping the piece next to it. Pick up the edge nearest you and roll to the other end. Stand the roll on its end and slightly open the top out so it resembles a rose. Serve with a wasabi leaf as garnish.

Lemon curls: Use a lemon zester to thinly shred and curl lemon peel for decoration.

Seasonal garnishes: Use a sprig of leaves or herbs or a small spray of blossom as a seasonal decoration on the plate, at the place settings or as a chopstick rest.

Simple leaf garnish: Arrange condiments on a fresh washed leaf—shiso, camellia, lemon—for a very simple but effective decoration.

Triangular lemon twists: Cut a slit halfway through each end of a rectangular slice of peel approximately 1 inch by ½ inch (2.5 cm by 12 mm), not quite opposite each other. Trim any excess, then twist so the pieces form an open triangle. Also suitable for limes, oranges, cucumber and carrot.

Vegetable flowers: Cut a 2-inch (5-cm) piece of peeled daikon and carrot. Place on end and cut out using a knife or a decorative flower-shaped biscuit cutter. Thinly slice both inside and outside sections of both vegetables to use as an edible garnish or in soups. For a more elaborate garnish, put carrot slices in a daikon surround and daikon slices in a carrot surround.

Wasabi leaf: Add enough water to wasabi powder to make a soft, spreadable paste. Roll about a teaspoon of wasabi paste or fresh wasabi into a small ball. Gently flatten and shape with fingers into a leaf shape. Using a knife or toothpick, lightly mark a central vein down the middle and side veins at a 45 degree angle. Place next to a ginger rose for guests to help themselves.

CUCUMBER CURLS

CUCUMBER DECORATION

RADISH CUPS

DECORATIVE CAMELLIA LEAVES

GINGER ROSE

LEMON CURLS

SEASONAL ROSEMARY GARNISH

SIMPLE LEAF GARNISH

TRIANGULAR LEMON TWISTS

DAIKON & CARROT FLOWERS

WASABI LEAF

VEGETARIAN SUSHI GARNISHES

Bamboo mat (makisu): Used to make sushi rolls and to drain leafy vegetables such as spinach and cabbage. Different sizes available, including half-sized for making hand-rolled sushi (temaki-zushi).

Wash in warm soapy water after use, using a kitchen brush to remove any rice from between the bamboo slats. Rinse well in cold water and stand mat on its end to drain and air-dry before storing.

Chopsticks (hashi): Japanese chopsticks have more pointed ends than the Chinese variety. Ornate, lacquered versions and inexpensive, disposable pine or bamboo, often in paper sleeves are available. Longer chopsticks are used for cooking and are usually joined at the top with string so they can be hung up.

Grater: Japanese graters grate more finely and evenly than most western graters and are especially suitable for fresh wasabi. Use fine graters for ginger—gently squeeze ginger to obtain ginger juice. Use a pastry brush to remove ginger from around the grater teeth and also to clean the grater. Alternatively, place a sheet of baking paper over the teeth before grating. Simply lift paper off and ginger comes with it.

Knives: Japanese knives are made of carbon steel, which provides a sharp edge but rusts easily, or stainless steel, which is less sharp but does not rust. For chopping and slicing vegetables use a long, square-bladed cleaver or very sharp western kitchen knives.

Mortar and pestle (suribachi & surikogi): Japanese mortars have a textured grooved pattern on an unglazed interior. This works like the surface of a grater when struck with a pestle. Japanese mortars are easier to use than conventional, smooth-surfaced mortars. Use the tip of a bamboo skewer to clean the grooves.

Omelette pan (maki yaki nabe): Traditionally square or rectangular, some for home-use have a nonstick surface. Used to make seasoned omelette (tamago-yaki) or thin omelette (usuyaki tamago). Season pan with oil before use. Clean pan after use by wiping with oil and rubbing with a clean cloth or paper towel. Do not scrub with any abrasive material and do not use the pan for any other use. A round frying pan or skillet can be substituted; simply trim omelette to required square shape.

Plates: Sushi plates should be as flat as possible, preferably without a rim.

Rice cooker: Automatic electric or gas rice cookers are highly recommended as rice is cooked to perfection every time. Some cookers have a "Keep Warm" button which maintains cooked rice temperature at a safe level until required. Be sure to turn cooker onto "Cook," not "Keep Warm" when ready to cook, as it can be confusing with two buttons.

Rice cup: Usually supplied with a rice cooker, the 6-fl oz (180-ml) cup measures 5 oz (150 g) rice and water for cooking rice. Water levels marked on inside of rice cooker relate to number of rice cups used.

Rice molds: See sushi molds.

Rice paddle (shamoji): This flat paddle is made of wood or plastic, and is often supplied with rice cooker. Because it is flat it can slice through rice when mixing without squashing the grains. A wooden spoon can be substituted. Dip in water with a splash of vinegar before use or the rice will stick.

Rice tub (handai/hangiri): Shallow, wooden tub traditionally made of cypress, is used to mix sushi rice or serve rice at the table. The wood absorbs excess moisture and keeps the rice warm. Various sizes are available but can be expensive. A wide, shallow dish or wooden salad bowl can be substituted, but not metal as it reacts with the sushi vinegar and gives the rice an unpleasant metallic taste.

Wash well after use and air-dry, leaving it to stand until completely dry. Store in a cool, dry place.

Shredder/slicer: A Japanese shredder has a selection of three blades to vary width and an adjustable dial to alter the depth of shredding. Use the wide blade to julienne vegetables, narrow blade to shred daikon and carrot for garnishes. Remove blades to use as a slicer. Larger and circular shredders are also available for shredding long continuous shreds.

Sushi mat: See bamboo mat.

Sushi Molds: Usually wood or plastic for home use, available in different shapes and sizes. Dip molds in water with a splash of rice vinegar to stop sushi rice sticking to mold.

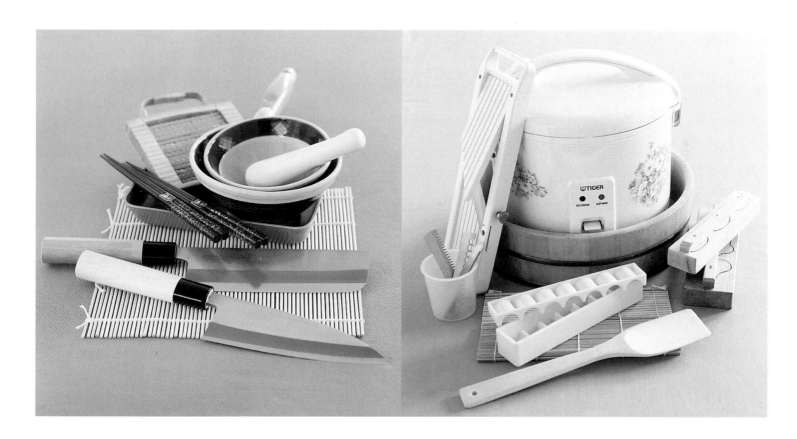

etiquette

- Green tea is normally served at the beginning and then throughout a meal.

- It is acceptable practice to slurp hot tea and soup as a sign of enjoyment and to blow on the liquid to cool.

- When giving or receiving food it is polite to use both hands when lifting the bowl or plate.

- Place chopsticks in front of guests, side by side, with both points on a chopstick rest facing to the left. Chopsticks that face to the right are a symbol of bad luck.

- The tips of chopsticks should never touch the table. Always use chopstick rests, which can be as simple as a folded napkin or the paper sleeve from the chopsticks.

- If using new, disposable wooden or bamboo chopsticks, have diners split apart and scrape one against the other to remove any splinters before use.

- Where possible, garnishes and table decorations should reflect the season.

- If no serving ware is provided, diners should use the handle end of individual chopsticks to take food from a communal dish. They then set the sushi onto their individual plate.

- Japanese plates rarely match in the manner of a Western dinner service. Plates are chosen for color, shape and texture to compliment the food served.

- Never fill serving platters, individual plates or dipping bowls to capacity, as this is considered rude. Be prepared to refill dipping bowls as needed.

- A Japanese meal is normally served all at once rather than in courses. Small portions are taken from platters at random. While anything not liked can be left, it is considered bad manners to leave any rice on the plate because rice is held in such high regard and has been the main food of Japan for centuries.

- It is quite acceptable to eat sushi with fingers. In Japan sushi is sometimes served without chopsticks as it is assumed fingers only will be used.

- Lift nigiri-zushi (see page 60) upside down if eaten with fingers or on its side if eaten with chopsticks. Dip the topping in sauce so it comes in contact with taste buds first, followed by the seasoned rice.

- You should never pour your own drinks. Offer to serve others and wait for someone to offer to fill your cup or if someone fills your cup, do likewise for them.

- An empty glass or cup means you would like a refill. If you don't want any more leave it full.

- Sake is to the Japanese as wine is to the French. There are different sakes of different grades. Drink sweet or dry heated to 105–120°F (40–50°C) or chilled.

- Always lift the sake cup when it is being filled from the sake bottle.

- Moisten and wring out a small hand towel, heat in the microwave or in a bamboo steamer and offer at the beginning and end of a Japanese meal for guests to refresh themselves.

Nori

To toast nori: Toasting nori is only required if not purchased toasted or if it needs to be freshened up. Place nori under the broiler (grill) or over a gas burner until crisp, for 30 seconds to a minute. Only one side needs to be toasted. If nori looses its crispness, it can be lightly toasted over a low heat.

To store nori: Light will affect the flavor and color of nori. Keep nori in a cool dark place. Once opened, packages should be wrapped in plastic wrap, foil or freezer bags, or kept in an airtight container, without any contact with moisture. Open packets can be refrigerated for one month or frozen for 3–4 months. Although they can still be used after this time, optimum flavor may be lost.

To drain leafy vegetables

Lay vegetables such as cabbage and spinach evenly across one end of a bamboo mat, roll firmly and squeeze gently to remove excess moisture.

To toast sesame seeds and nuts

Place seeds or nuts in a dry frying pan and cook over moderate heat until golden. Stir constantly as they can burn easily. Toasted sesame seeds are available from Asian food stores.

Seasoned kampyo

1 oz (30 g) kampyo

1 cup (8 fl oz/250 ml) dashi stock or
    water (see page 101)

2 tablespoons sugar

2 teaspoons sake

2 tablespoons soy sauce

Wash kampyo in cold water and salt, gently rubbing the strips together. Drain and wash again. Alternatively, soak in water to soften for 2 hours or longer. Place kampyo and water in a saucepan and gently boil until tender, about 10 minutes. Drain well. In a saucepan, bring kampyo, dashi, sugar, sake and soy sauce to a boil. Reduce heat and simmer for 15 minutes. Remove from heat and cool in liquid. Drain and cut into 8-inch (20-cm) lengths.

Makes 18

SEASONED KAMPYO

Seasoned carrots

1 medium carrot, peeled and cut into
    thin strips

1/3 cup (3 fl oz/90 ml) dashi stock or
    water (see page 101)

2 teaspoons sugar

1 teaspoon light soy sauce

pinch salt

In a small saucepan combine dashi, sugar, soy sauce and salt. Simmer over low heat until carrot is tender and most of the liquid is absorbed. Remove using a slotted spoon and set aside to cool.

Hint

Other vegetables can be substituted in these recipes, but cooking times may vary. Adjust seasonings to personal taste.

SEASONED CARROTS

Seasoned shiitake mushrooms

6 dried shiitake mushrooms

¹/₂ cup (4 fl oz/125 ml) dashi stock or water (see page 101)

1¹/₂ tablespoons caster sugar

1¹/₂ tablespoons soy sauce

2 tablespoons mirin

Cover mushrooms in warm water until softened, 20–30 minutes. Remove using a slotted spoon. Use seasoned liquid in soups and other dishes. Discard stems and slice thinly or keep mushroom caps whole, depending on use. Place in a saucepan with remaining ingredients and simmer for 10 minutes. Remove using a slotted spoon. Use seasoned liquid to flavor cooked rice.

SEASONED SHIITAKE MUSHROOMS

Seasoned lotus root

2 oz (60 g) lotus root, peeled and cut into ¹/₈-inch (5-mm) slices

2 tablespoons sugar

3 tablespoons rice vinegar

¹/₂ teaspoon salt

Soak lotus root water and rice vinegar to prevent discoloration. In a saucepan, bring remaining ingredients to a boil. Add the lotus slices and simmer for 8–10 minutes. Drain.

SEASONED LOTUS ROOTS

Thick seasoned omelette
(Tamago-yaki)

8 large eggs, lightly beaten

2 tablespoons dashi stock or water
  (see page 101)

2 tablespoons sugar

1 tablespoon mirin

1 tablespoon light soy sauce

1/4 teaspoon salt

1-2 tablespoons vegetable oil

1/2 cup (3/4 oz/20 g) grated daikon, drained

Japanese soy sauce

Combine eggs, dashi, sugar, mirin, soy sauce and salt in a bowl, stirring well until sugar dissolves, and divide mixture in half. Heat an 8-inch (20-cm) square omelette pan, small frying pan or skillet over moderate-low heat. Coat with a thin layer of oil, wiping excess with paper towel. Cover frying pan thinly with egg mixture, tilting pan to spread evenly to each corner. Break any air bubbles with chopsticks so omelette lies flat. When almost set, run chopsticks around the edges to loosen egg from pan, then lift egg on the side furthest away from you and fold into thirds towards the front of the pan. Gently push folded omelette to back of pan. Lightly grease pan with paper towel and repeat the procedure, lifting up cooked egg so mixture runs underneath. When nearly cooked, fold in thirds starting with the egg already folded. Repeat for remaining mixture lightly greasing pan between batches.

While hot, tip omelette onto a bamboo mat and wrap firmly, forming a compact rectangular shape. Cool and cut as required. Repeat with remaining half mixture. Serve with daikon and soy sauce.

Makes 2 omelettes

Thin seasoned omelette
(Usuyaki tamago)

6 eggs

1 tablespoon mirin

1 tablespoon sugar

1/4 teaspoon salt

1-2 teaspoons vegetable oil

Gently beat eggs with mirin, sugar and salt, without creating big air bubbles. Strain mixture to remove any strands of egg. Lightly grease an 8-inch (20-cm) square or 9-inch (23-cm) round frying pan or skillet with oil, wiping any excess with paper towel. Heat oiled pan on moderate-low until a drop of water flicked onto surface skips across surface and evaporates quickly.

Cover frying pan thinly with egg mixture, tilting pan to spread evenly into each corner. Break any air bubbles with chopsticks so omelette lies flat. When almost set and surface begins to look firm and slightly dry, run chopsticks around edges to loosen egg from pan. Flip omelette over and cook other side for only a few seconds, being careful not to overcook. Remove to a plate. Repeat for remaining mixture, lightly greasing pan between each batch. If a round frying pan is used, omelettes may be trimmed to a square shape as required.

Makes about 8 omelettes

Tips

To use for nigiri-zushi, cut omelette across into 1/2-inch (12-mm) slices or cut lengthwise into long thin strips, 1/2 inch (12 mm) wide, to use as a filling for sushi rolls.

To use as a side dish to accompany sushi, serve seasoned omelette with soy sauce and grated daikon .

sushi rice

Sushi rice

3 cups (20 oz/600 g) uncooked short
grain rice

3–3¹/₄ cups (24–27 fl oz/750–815 ml)
water depending on age of rice
and texture preference
(see notes below)

SUSHI VINEGAR

8 tablespoons (3.5 fl oz/120 ml)
rice vinegar

4 tablespoons sugar

¹/₂ teaspoon salt

Makes about ¹/₂ cup (4 fl oz/125 ml)

Makes about 9 cups (45 oz/1.35 L) or about 3 lb (1.5 kg) depending on how densely rice was packed.

For additional flavor, add a piece of konbu or sake to the rice while it is cooking. For variety, add grated lemon zest, finely chopped fresh herbs, roasted nuts, toasted sesame seeds, pickled vegetables, wakame (seaweed) or finely grated fresh ginger to cooked sushi rice.

Brown sushi rice

2 cups (13 oz/400 g) uncooked short
grain brown rice

2³/₄–3 cups water (22–24 fl
oz/685–750 ml), depending on age
of rice and texture preference
(see notes below)

SUSHI VINEGAR

¹/₄ cup (2 fl oz/60 ml) rice vinegar

2 tablespoons sugar

¹/₄ teaspoon salt

Although short grain brown rice does not cling as easily as short grain white rice, its nutty flavor and chewier texture make an interesting alternative.

Rinse brown rice once and cook as white sushi rice until most liquid is absorbed, about 30–35 minutes. Remove from heat and stand, covered, 10–15 minutes longer. Combine ingredients of sushi vinegar, stir into rice and fan to cool.

Tips for making perfect sushi rice

1. To successfully make sushi rice, choose short or medium grain rice, which has the right texture, taste and consistency to gently cling together without being too sticky when cooked.

2. A rice cooker is highly recommended as it produces perfect rice every time. The absorption method in a saucepan or microwave also works well, but avoid the rapid boil method.

3. Rinse rice 3–4 times before cooking to remove excess surface starch that could make the rice too sticky. Drain for 15 minutes.

4. Cool warm rice using an electric fan on lowest setting.

5. The standard rice cup provided with a rice cooker = 1 cup (5 oz/150 g) uncooked rice; 1 metric cup (8 fl oz/250 ml) = about 1¹/₃ cup (7 oz/200 g) uncooked rice. For accuracy, be sure to use the same cup to measure rice and water. Or follow manufacturer's instructions.

6. The texture of cooked rice is a matter of taste and varies with the age and storage conditions of uncooked rice. For a softer rice texture, cook the rice with a little more water. For a firmer texture, decrease the water amount.

7. Sushi rice is cooked with slightly less water than rice served as a side dish. It is slightly firmer and chewier than plain steamed rice.

1. Put rice in a bowl, fill with cold water and mix gently with hand. Drain and repeat 2–3 times until water is nearly clear.

2. Leave rice under cold running water for a few minutes.

3. Drain well for 15–30 minutes or put rice and measured water in rice cooker or saucepan and let stand for 30 minutes before cooking.

4. To make sushi vinegar: Combine vinegar, sugar and salt, stirring well until sugar dissolves. Mixture can be gently heated to dissolve sugar and make the vinegar slightly milder. Set aside until required.

5. To cook rice in a rice cooker: Measure rice in rice cup provided. After rinsing put rice in rice cooker and add water to the required cup measurement marked on inside of bowl in rice cooker. Cover and switch to cook. When cooker automatically switches to keep warm let stand with lid on to complete cooking process, 10 minutes.

6. To cook rice in a saucepan: In a medium saucepan bring rinsed rice and water to a boil. Reduce heat and simmer, covered, on low heat until all water is absorbed, 12–15 minutes.

7. Remove from heat and let stand with lid on to complete the cooking process, 10–15 minutes. Note: rice can also be cooked in the microwave or steamed in a bamboo steamer.

8. Spread rice out in a large, preferably flat-bottomed, nonmetallic bowl or tub.

9. Using a rice paddle or wooden spoon, slice through rice at a 45 degree angle to break up any lumps, while slowly pouring sushi vinegar over rice to distribute evenly. Not all the vinegar may be needed.

10. Continue to slice, not stir as it squashes the grains, lifting and turning the rice from the outside into the center.

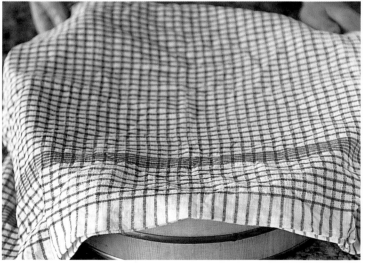

11. Fan the rice so it cools to body temperature, turning occasionally, 5–8 minutes. Cooling gives good flavor, texture and gloss to the rice. If rice becomes too cold it hardens; do not refrigerate.

12. Keep covered with a damp cloth to stop rice drying out while making sushi. Alternatively, keep in a nonstick surface rice cooker.

Temaki-zushi

5 cups (25 oz/780 g) Sushi rice (see page 28
   for recipe)

8 sheets nori

1 tablespoon wasabi paste

2–3 fillings per roll (see list below)

2–3 tablespoons gari

1/2 cup (4 fl oz/125 ml) Japanese soy sauce

Suggested fillings

Avocado, bell peppers, capers, shredded carrot, cucumber strips, kimchee, shredded lettuce, seasoned omelette, pickled radish (takuan), snow pea sprouts, blanched asparagus, blanched spinach, snow peas (mange-tout), snow pea sprouts, seasoned kampyo, toasted sesame seeds, wasabi mayonnaise, natto (fermented soybeans), shiso, scallion and Japanese mustard.

For seafood-eating vegetarians, some options are: Smoked salmon with avocado, onion slices and capers, or sashimi tuna with wasabi mayonnaise and snow pea sprouts. If desired, substitute nori with katsuo sheets (dried bonito).

These do-it-yourself hand-rolled cones are a great idea for a party and very easy for the host. Prepare ingredients beforehand, placing them on a platter or in individual bowls. Give your guests guidance on technique, and let them make their own. Hand-rolled sushi should be eaten as soon as made as they do not hold well. Prepare a finger bowl with water and a splash of rice vinegar for each person. Provide warmed, dampened towels for guests to wipe their hands on.

To Prepare: Put sushi rice in a nonmetallic bowl and cover with a damp cloth. Cut nori sheets into quarters and cover with plastic wrap until ready to serve or they will absorb moisture from the atmosphere, and become soft and wrinkled. Cones can be made with half sheets of nori, if preferred. Sushi rice can be premeasured just before required to make it easier for guests to handle. Use an ice cream scoop, dipped in vinegar and water, so rice doesn't stick, to measure rice and place on a tray covered with plastic wrap or damp cloth. Prepare a selection of fillings and arrange on a platter with wasabi, gari and soy sauce in separate bowls.

To serve: Place a quarter sheet of nori diagonally in the palm of one hand, shiny side down. Dip fingers of other hand in vinegar and water, shaking off excess. Place 1–2 tablespoons rice in center of nori and spread towards top corner, making a slight groove down middle of rice for fillings. Spread wasabi lightly down groove and top with fillings. Fold one side of nori over so it sticks to rice. Fold other side of nori over the first to form a cone. To hold cone shape securely, fold back tip of cone. Dip in soy sauce and add gari as desired.

Makes 32

Tempura sushi roll

(Tempura maki-zushi)

3 cups (24 fl oz/750 ml) vegetable oil for
   deep frying

TEMPURA BATTER

1 egg yolk

$^1/_2$ cup (3 fl oz/90 ml) iced water

$^1/_2$ cup (2 oz/60 g) sifted all-purpose (plain) flour
   plus extra flour for dusting

TEMPURA VEGETABLES

1 carrot, cut into thin strips 2 inches (5 cm) long

3 oz (90 g) green beans, ends trimmed and halved

red, green or yellow bell pepper (capsicum), cut
   into thin strips 2 inches (5 cm) long

FOR SUSHI CONES

2–3 cups (10–15 oz/300–450 g) Sushi rice (see page
   28 for recipe)

4–6 sheets nori, halved

8 shiso or small lettuce leaves, shredded or
   cucumber strips (optional)

DIPPING SAUCE

$^1/_2$ cup (4 fl oz/125 ml) Dashi I (see page 101
   for recipe) or stock

2 tablespoons light soy sauce

1 tablespoon mirin

$^1/_4$ cup (2 oz/60 g) grated fresh daikon (optional)

1 teaspoon peeled and grated fresh ginger

To make tempura vegetables: Pour oil in a large saucepan or deep fryer and heat until moderately hot (325°F/170°C). While oil is heating, prepare the batter. Place egg yolk in a bowl and add iced water, mixing lightly, without beating or creating air bubbles. Add measured flour at once and mix until just combined but still lumpy. Lightly dust vegetables in additional flour, shaking off excess, then dip in batter. Deep fry until golden, 2–3 minutes. Serve immediately.

To make sushi cones: Place 1–2 tablespoons sushi rice on the short end of half nori sheet. Add a tempura vegetable and a lettuce leaf and roll nori around the fillings. Serve immediately. Guests dip cone into dipping sauce and eat.

To make dipping sauce: Heat dashi, soy sauce and mirin over low heat. Pour into individual dipping bowls. Gently squeeze excess liquid from daikon and place in middle of sauce, topped with ginger.

Makes 8–12 cones

TEMPURA SUSHI ROLL (TEMPURA MAKI-ZUSHI)

sushi rolls

Norimaki

There are many variations of sushi rolls, but basically they are divided into thin rolls (hosomaki) or thick rolls (futomaki) depending on whether a half or whole sheet of nori is used. Norimaki refers to sushi rolls (maki-zushi) that are wrapped in nori.

Hints

1. Although you can use plastic wrap, foil or waxed paper to make sushi rolls, a bamboo mat makes the job much easier. They are relatively inexpensive to purchase and should last well if properly cared for. Don't cut sushi rolls on the mat as knife may cut through string.

2. Keep spare pieces of nori covered and dry while making sushi as they absorb moisture from the atmosphere and will be difficult to roll.

3. Nori will shrink slightly as it becomes moist from the rice. Be careful not to overfill rolls as they may be difficult to close or may split open. Make thicker rolls by turning the whole sheet of nori vertically on the bamboo mat so short side is nearest you, and using more fillings.

4. For interesting variations use food coloring, beet (beetroot) liquid, finely diced vegetables or herbs to color rice.

5. Use one or two fillings in small rolls and five or six in large. If using more fillings, cut the ingredients thinner so rolls do not burst open.

6. Have a finger bowl handy when making rolls to dip fingers in so rice does not stick. Finger bowl is water with a splash of rice vinegar.

7. To keep fillings in center, either build a small mound of rice along edge of rice on the long side farthest away from you nearest the nori strip or make a small impression across the center of the rice with fingers where fillings will be placed.

8. Serve sushi with gari and Japanese soy sauce for dipping. Traditionally, dipping bowls are small and never filled to capacity. Refresh dipping bowls often as bits of rice often end up in the dish, which looks unappetizing.

9. When sushi is made with wasabi, serve extra on the side so it can be added to taste. Although it is a matter of personal taste, traditionally wasabi is not used with seasoned or pickled ingredients.

10. If making sushi for a mixed crowd, especially children, it may be advisable to make some without wasabi.

11. Consume rolls within a couple of hours of preparation. Cut pieces as close to serving time as possible so rice does not dry out; cover with plastic wrap.

12. Cut some rolls on the diagonal for variety of presentation. Cut each roll in half, then half again. Cut each remaining piece in half at a 45-degree angle. Stand these pieces up for presentation.

Sushi roll troubleshooting

There are never any mistakes when making sushi, just new designs! Sushi chefs over the centuries have discovered these solutions to common problems.

Fillings of sushi rolls are off-center

Reason: Fillings fell forward as mat was rolled and ended up on the edge of the rice.

Solution: Once the roll is cut, use fingers to gently shape each sushi piece into a tear drop with filling at the narrow end. Arrange pieces in a circle with fillings towards the center, add a garnish to the middle and you have a sushi flower.

Roll splits open

Reason: Too much rice or filling or both.

Solution: If roll is overfilled and starts to split open, do not cut into pieces. Place another ½ sheet of nori (for thin rolls) or full sheet (for large rolls) on bamboo mat, shiny side down. Place roll with split facing down onto nori. Lightly dampen along both long sides of nori and roll up with bamboo mat, away from you, as for a sushi roll. Cut into 6 or 8 pieces from the middle first.

Alternatively, use a split thin roll as the filling for a larger roll. Lay a whole sheet of nori on the bamboo mat and cover thinly with rice, leaving a ¾-inch (2-cm) strip on the far side uncovered. Place the split roll across rice and roll as for a sushi roll. (For variety, sprinkle rice with toasted sesame seeds, thinly sliced scallion (shallot/spring onion), wasabi mayonnaise or a thin layer of umeboshi plum, depending on the filling already used.

Extra rice

Reason: Forgot to leave a strip of nori with no rice.

Solution: Simply make an inside-out roll (see page 52 for recipe).

Cut the nori sheet the wrong way

Reason: When making a small sushi roll the nori is folded and cut parallel with the lines marked on the "rough" side. If cut the other way there is very little nori to cover the rice and filling.

Solution: Make it into Wisteria sushi (see page 82 for recipe), an inside-out roll (see page 52 for recipe) or use less rice and thinner fillings to make a thinner sushi roll.

Making sushi rolls takes too long

Reason: You didn't want to do all the work and you wanted your party to include entertainment.

Solution: Get everybody to make their own sushi. Prepare ingredients for hand-rolled sushi (temaki-zushi, see page 32) and sushi pouches (see page 64). Alternatively, serve buffet-style sushi (chirashi-zushi), arranging sushi ingredients in layers in a decorative box, dish or plate (see page 90). Making these types of sushi is simple and is great fun.

Cucumber and sesame sushi rolls

(Hosomaki-zushi)

3 sheets nori

3 cups (15 oz/450 g) Sushi rice (see recipe page 28)

1 teaspoon wasabi paste

2 tablespoons toasted white sesame seeds

1 English (hothouse) or telegraph cucumber,
   seeded and thinly sliced lengthwise

1 tablespoon gari

$^1/_4$ cup (2 fl oz/60 ml) Japanese soy sauce

finger bowl: water with a splash of rice vinegar

Cut each nori sheet in half lengthwise, parallel with the lines marked on the rough side. Place one half nori sheet lengthwise on a bamboo mat about 3 slats from the edge closest to you, shiny side down. Dip both hands in finger bowl, shaking off excess. Spread one sixth of rice evenly over nori, leaving a ¾-inch (2-cm) strip on long side farthest away uncovered. Gently rake fingers across grains to spread rice.

Build a small mound of rice along edge nearest the uncovered nori strip to help keep fillings in place.

Spread a pinch of wasabi across center of rice. Sprinkle with sesame seeds and arrange one third of cucumber strips, making sure they extend completely to each end. Using your index finger and thumb, pick up edge of mat nearest you. Place remaining fingers over fillings to hold them in as you roll forward, tightly wrapping rice and nori around fillings. The strip of nori without rice should still be visible.

Press gently and continue rolling forward to complete roll. Gently press mat to shape and seal roll. Unroll mat and place roll on chopping board with seam on bottom. Wipe a sharp knife with a damp cloth and cut roll in half. Pick up one half roll and turn it 180 degrees so cut ends of rolls are on the same side. Cut rolls to make 6 pieces, wiping knife between each cut. Repeat for remaining rolls. Serve with remaining wasabi, gari and Japanese soy sauce.

Makes 6 rolls (36 pieces)

Variations

Grilled shiitake brushed with teriyaki sauce (see page 105) or marinated vegetables (see page 105 for marinade).

Radish and kampyo rolls
(Hosomaki-zushi)

3 sheets nori

3 cups (15 oz/450 g) Sushi rice (see page 28)

6 strips pickled radish (takuan), $\frac{1}{2}$ inch by $\frac{1}{2}$
  inch by $7\frac{1}{4}$ inches (1 cm by 1 cm by 18.5 cm)

6 pieces Seasoned kampyo (see page 24)

1 teaspoon wasabi

1 tablespoon gari

$\frac{1}{4}$ cup (2 fl oz/60 ml) Japanese soy sauce

finger bowl: water with a splash of rice vinegar

Prepare rolls as for Cucumber rolls (see page 38 for recipe), using one strip pickled radish and kampyo per roll and eliminating wasabi. (Note: traditionally, wasabi is not used with pickled vegetables, but serve on the side for guests to add to taste.)

Serve with wasabi, gari and Japanese soy sauce.

Makes 6 rolls (36 pieces)

Spinach and pine nut rolls
(Hosomaki-zushi)

5 oz (150 g) spinach leaves, blanched and
  well drained

$\frac{1}{2}$ teaspoon Asian sesame oil

3 sheets nori

3 cups (15 oz/450 g) Sushi rice (see page 28)

1 teaspoon wasabi paste

2 tablespoons toasted pine nuts

1 tablespoon gari

$\frac{1}{4}$ cup (2 fl oz/60 ml) Japanese soy sauce

finger bowl: water with a splash of rice vinegar

Chop blanched spinach finely and mix with sesame oil. Prepare rolls as for Cucumber rolls (see recipe page 38) using spinach and pine nuts as fillings. Serve wasabi, gari and Japanese soy sauce separately.

To toast pine nuts: Place in a dry frying pan and cook over moderate heat, stirring continuously until nuts are golden.

Makes 6 rolls (36 pieces)

Variation

Substitute pine nuts with toasted sesame seeds. Or add thin strips of seasoned tempeh or strips of Seasoned tofu (see page 64).

RADISH AND KAMPYO ROLLS (HOSOMAKI-ZUSHI)

Asparagus and sweet red pepper sushi rolls

(Hosomaki-zushi)

FOR SESAME DRESSING

2 tablespoons white sesame seeds or tahini

2 teaspoons Japanese soy sauce to taste

2 teaspoons sugar

6 thin asparagus, blanched

1/3 red bell pepper (capsicum), seeded and
  thinly sliced

3 sheets nori

3 cups (15 oz/450 g) Sushi rice (see page 28)

2 tablespoons gari, for garnish

1/4 cup (2 fl oz/60 ml) Japanese soy sauce,
  for serving

To make dressing: Place sesame seeds in a dry frying pan over moderate heat until golden and seeds begin to jump. Grind in a mortar and pestle to a smooth paste. (Alternatively, use tahini.) Combine with soy sauce and sugar, stirring until sugar dissolves. If mixture is too thick, add a little water, stock or sake.

Prepare rolls as for Cucumber rolls (see recipe page 38), using sesame dressing, asparagus and red pepper strips as fillings. Garnish with gari and serve with soy sauce.

Makes 6 rolls (36 pieces)

Variations

1. *Umeboshi plums or plum paste and shiso leaves. Shiso can be used whole wrapped around plums or finely chopped and sprinkled on or through rice.*

2. *Seasoned kampyo (see page 24), toasted sesame seeds, sprinkle of shichimi togarashi (7 chili spice).*

Seafood options: Thin strips of cucumber and sashimi tuna. Smoked salmon and dill mayonnaise.

Step-by-step large sushi rolls
(Futomaki-zushi)

4 sheets nori

4 cups (20 oz/600 g) Sushi rice (see recipe
page 28)

2 teaspoons wasabi paste

FOR FILLINGS

4 strips Seasoned kampyo (see page 24)

1/2 English (hothouse) cucumber, seeded and
thinly sliced

4 strips Thick seasoned omelette (see page 26)

4 strips pickled radish (takuan)

2 tablespoons beni-shoga

1/4 cup (2 fl oz/60 ml) Japanese soy sauce

finger bowl: water with a splash of rice vinegar

Place long side of one nori sheet lengthwise on bamboo mat about 3 slats from the edge closest to you, shiny side down. Dip both hands in finger bowl, shaking off excess. Working from one side to the other, spread one quarter of rice evenly over nori leaving a 1-inch (2.5-cm) strip uncovered on the long side farthest from you. Gently rake fingers across grains to spread rice evenly. Build a small mound of rice along edge nearest the uncovered nori strip to help keep fillings in place.

Spread a pinch of wasabi across center of rice then layer fillings, making sure each extends completely to both ends so there will be filling in the end pieces when cut. Using your index finger and thumb, pick up edge of bamboo mat nearest you. Place remaining fingers over fillings to hold them as you roll mat forward tightly, wrapping rice and nori around fillings. The strip of nori without rice should still be visible.

Press gently and continue rolling forward to complete roll. Gently press mat to shape and seal roll. Unroll mat and place roll on cutting board with seam on bottom.

Wipe a sharp knife with a damp cloth and cut roll in half. Pick up one half roll and turn it 180 degrees so cut ends are on the same side. Cut rolls in half, then in half again to make 8 pieces, wiping knife between each cut. Repeat for remaining rolls. Serve with remaining wasabi and Japanese soy sauce.

Makes 4 rolls (32 pieces)

Filling Variations

1. *Seasoned kampyo (see page 24), cucumber, omelette, pickled radish (takuan).*

2. *Beni-shoga, cucumber, omelette, sliced bamboo shoots, strips seasoned tofu or tempeh.*

3. *Cucumber, shredded carrot, red bell pepper (capsicum), avocado, toasted sesame seeds, seasoned shiitake mushrooms, scallions.*

4. *Tempura roll: Hot tempura vegetables, cucumber, shredded lettuce, wasabi, mayonnaise (or substitute wasabi and mayonnaise with sweet chili sauce).*

Seafood options: Japanese crab meat, sashimi tuna or salmon, denbu/oboro, or cooked shrimp.

Avocado-wasabi sushi canapes

2 sheets nori

2 cups (10 oz/300 g) Sushi rice (see page 28)

1 teaspoon wasabi paste

2 scallions (shallots/spring onions), green part only, thinly sliced

1/2 small avocado, peeled and thinly sliced

3/4 cup (1 1/2 oz/45 g) snow pea (mange-tout) sprouts, stems trimmed

2 tablespoons mayonnaise

These sushi rolls can be thickly or thinly sliced and used as a base to be decorated with favorite toppings. Prepare rolls as for Cucumber rolls (see recipe page 38) beginning with rice as a filling then scattering wasabi and scallions over rice. Cut roll thinly into about 1/2-inch (1-cm) pieces. Top each slice with a piece of avocado, snow pea sprouts and mayonnaise.

Makes 2 rolls (about 28 thin pieces)

Vegetarian California rolls

2 teaspoons wasabi

2 tablespoons mayonnaise

4 sheets nori

4 cups (20 oz/600 g) Sushi rice (see page 28)

1 English (hothouse) cucumber, seeded and thinly sliced

1 avocado, peeled and thinly sliced

1 carrot, coarsely shredded

1 cup (2 oz/60 g) snow pea (mange-tout) sprouts, stems trimmed

4 shiso or small lettuce leaves, shredded (optional)

2 tablespoons gari

1/4 cup (2 fl oz/60 ml) Japanese soy sauce

finger bowl: water with a splash of rice vinegar

In a small bowl, combine wasabi and mayonnaise. Prepare rolls as for Large sushi rolls (see page 44), spreading wasabi mayonnaise across the rice before adding other ingredients.

Makes 4 rolls (32 pieces)

Variations

Seafood options: Cooked prawn, crab meat, flying fish roe, sashimi tuna and salmon.

AVOCADO-WASABI SUSHI CANAPES

Omelette sushi rolls

5 Seasoned shiitake mushrooms (see page 24 for recipe), finely chopped

1 Seasoned carrot (see page 24 for recipe), peeled and julienned

2 Seasoned tofu, thinly sliced (see page 64)

2 cups (10 oz/315 g) Sushi rice (see page 28)

2 Thin seasoned omelettes (see page 26)

2 sheets nori

1 English (hothouse) cucumber, seeded and thinly sliced lengthwise

$^1/_4$ cup Japanese soy sauce, for serving

2 tablespoons gari, for serving

In a bowl, combine seasoned shiitake, seasoned carrot, seasoned tofu and rice, mixing well.

Cover a bamboo mat with a plastic wrap. Lay one omelette on plastic and cover with a sheet of nori. Spread nori with rice mixture, leaving a 1-inch (2.5-cm) strip on long side farthest away uncovered. Lay half cucumber strips across rice, making sure they extend to each end. Pick up mat and plastic with index finger and thumb, holding cucumber in place with remaining fingers and roll and seal nori around cucumber. Unroll mat and plastic. Place roll on cutting board with seam on bottom. Wipe a sharp knife with a damp cloth and cut roll into 8 pieces, wiping knife before each cut. Repeat for remaining roll. Serve with soy sauce and gari.

Makes 2 rolls (16 pieces)

Variations

1. *Use nori half sheets to make thin rolls.*

2. *Substitute blanched spinach or green beans for cucumber, and tempeh for seasoned tofu.*

OMELETTE SUSHI ROLLS

Pin wheel sushi rolls

(Futomaki-zushi)

4 sheets nori

4 cups (20 oz/600 g) Sushi rice (see page 28)

2 teaspoons wasabi paste

5–6 fillings per roll (see list below)

2 tablespoons gari

$^1/_4$ cup (2 fl oz/60 ml) Japanese soy sauce

finger bowl: water with a splash of rice vinegar

Make these sushi rolls the same way as Large sushi rolls (see page 44), except lay fillings across rice so when rolled ingredients and nori form a pin wheel pattern. Alternate different colored ingredients for different effects. Using the same ingredients, make Inside-out rolls (see page 52) with rice on the outside. Then, sprinkle rice with toasted sesame seeds or fresh herbs.

Place short side of one nori sheet lengthwise on bamboo mat about 3 slats from edge closest to you, shiny side down. Dip both hands in finger bowl, shaking off excess. Working from one side to the other, spread one quarter of rice evenly over nori leaving a 1-inch (2.5-cm) strip on the long side farthest from you uncovered. Gently rake fingers across grains to spread rice. Spread a pinch of wasabi across center of rice. Place fillings across rice next to each other, beginning about ¾ inch (2 cm) from edge nearest you and extending to within 1½ inches (4 cm) of opposite edge. Make sure fillings extend completely to each side or there will be no filling in end pieces when cut.

Using your index finger and thumb, pick up edge of bamboo mat nearest you. Roll forward straight down over first filling. Continue rolling forward to complete roll, pulling mat forward as you go so it does not get rolled in with rice. Gently press mat to shape roll. Unroll mat and place roll on cutting board with seam on bottom.

Wipe a sharp knife with a damp cloth and cut roll in half. Pick up one half roll and turn it 180 degrees so cut ends of rolls are on the same side. Cut rolls in half, then in half again to make 8 pieces, wiping knife with each cut. Repeat for remaining rolls. Serve with remaining wasabi, gari and Japanese soy sauce.

Makes 4 rolls (32 pieces)

Filling variations

1. *Mayonnaise, cucumber, avocado, snow pea (mange-tout) sprouts, or lettuce.*

2. *Cucumber, shredded carrot, bell pepper (capsicum), avocado, snow pea sprouts.*

3. *Seasoned shiitake mushrooms, omelette, cucumber, Seasoned kampyo, blanched spinach.*

4. *Seasoned kampyo, cucumber, omelette, pickled radish (takuan).*

Seafood options: Flying fish roe, cooked shrimp, or sashimi tuna, or canned tuna or salmon, denbu/oboro.

PIN WHEEL SUSHI ROLLS (FUTOMAKI-ZUSHI)

Inside-out sushi rolls

(Uramaki-zushi)

2 sheets nori

3 cups (15 oz/500 g) Sushi rice (see page 28)

1 tablespoon combined toasted black and white
sesame seeds

1–2 tablespoons wasabi paste

1/2 English (hothouse) or telegraph cucumber,
seeded and thinly sliced

4 strips Seasoned kampyo (see page 24)

2 tablespoons beni-shoga

8 snow peas (mange-tout), blanched and
thinly sliced

1/2 red bell pepper (capsicum), seeded and
thinly sliced

1/4 cup (2 fl oz/60 ml) Japanese soy sauce

finger bowl: water with a splash of rice vinegar

Cut each piece of nori in half lengthwise, parallel with lines marked on rough side. Place one half nori sheet along long side of a bamboo mat nearest you. Dip both hands in finger bowl, shaking off excess. Spread one quarter of rice evenly over nori. Gently rake fingers across grains to spread rice. Sprinkle rice with mixed sesame seeds and cover with a large sheet of plastic wrap.

Pick up mat, carefully turn over so nori is now on top and place back on mat about 3 slats from edge closest to you. Spread a pinch of wasabi and selection of fillings across center of nori. Make sure fillings extend completely to each end. Using your index finger and thumb, pick up edge of bamboo mat and plastic wrap nearest you. Place remaining fingers over fillings to hold them as you roll mat forward tightly, wrapping rice and nori around fillings.

Press gently and continue rolling forward to complete roll. Gently press mat to shape and seal roll. Unroll mat and plastic.

Wipe a sharp knife with a damp cloth and cut roll in half. Cut each half in half twice more to make 8 pieces, wiping knife with each cut. Repeat with remaining roll. Serve with remaining wasabi and Japanese soy sauce.

Makes 4 rolls (32 pieces)

Filling Variations

1. *Cucumber, avocado, seasoned tempeh and sesame seeds.*

2. *Red bell pepper, red pickled ginger, snow pea sprouts and cucumber.*

3. *Shredded carrot, avocado, scallion, snow pea sprouts and horseradish cream.*

Seafood coatings might include: denbu/oboro (flaked fish), bonito flakes or flying fish roe.

Seafood options: Sashimi salmon, cucumber, avocado and sesame seeds, or smoked salmon, wasabi mayonnaise, avocado, scallion and asparagus.

INSIDE-OUT SUSHI ROLLS (URAMAKI-ZUSHI) 5 3

Spinach brown rice sushi rolls with miso sesame

5 oz (150 g) spinach leaves, blanched and
   drained well

$^{1}/_{2}$ teaspoon Japanese soy sauce

2 scallions (shallots/spring onions), green part
   only, finely chopped

1 tablespoon toasted white sesame seeds (see page
   23 for instructions)

2 sheets nori

2 cups (10 oz/300 g) Brown sushi rice
   (see page 28)

Miso sesame dipping sauce (see recipe page 104)

finger bowl: water with a splash of rice vinegar

Chop spinach leaves finely and sprinkle with soy sauce. Cut each piece nori in half lengthwise, parallel with lines marked on the rough side.

Fold scallions and sesame seeds into rice until evenly distributed. Place one half nori sheet lengthwise on bamboo mat, about 3 slats from edge closest to you, shiny side down. Dip both hands in finger bowl, shaking off excess. Spread one quarter of rice evenly over nori, leaving a $^{3}/_{4}$-inch (2-cm) strip uncovered on long side farthest from you. Carefully make a lengthwise groove in middle of rice. Add a layer of spinach, making sure it extends evenly to each end. Using your index finger and thumb, pick up edge of the bamboo mat nearest you. Place remaining fingers over fillings to hold them as you roll mat forward, tightly wrapping rice and nori around fillings. The strip of nori without rice should still be visible.

Press firmly and continue rolling forward to complete roll. Gently press mat to shape roll. Unroll mat and place roll on cutting board with seam on bottom. Wipe a knife with a damp cloth and cut roll into 6 pieces, wiping knife with each cut. Repeat with remaining roll. Serve with Miso sesame sauce.

Makes 4 rolls (24 pieces)

Tip

Roll firmly when using brown rice.

Pickled plum and brown rice sushi rolls

1 tablespoon vegetable oil

2 carrots, peeled and cut lengthwise into
thin strips

1 clove garlic, ground (minced)

1 teaspoon peeled and grated fresh ginger

2 eggs, lightly beaten

1 tablespoon Japanese soy sauce

1 tablespoon umeboshi plum paste

1 tablespoon rice vinegar

4 sheets nori

4 cups (20 oz/625 g) Brown sushi rice (see recipe
page 28)

4 scallions (shallots/spring onions), green
parts only

1/4 cup (2 fl oz/60 ml) Japanese soy sauce

finger bowl: water with a splash of rice vinegar

Heat oil in frying pan over moderate heat and sauté carrot, garlic and ginger until carrots are just cooked, about 2 minutes. Remove from pan. Combine eggs and tablespoon of soy sauce and spread thinly over frying pan. Cook until just set, about 45 seconds. Turn over and cook about 20 seconds longer. Remove from pan and slice into thin strips. Combine plum paste and vinegar and gently fold into rice.

Place a sheet of nori lengthwise on bamboo mat, about 3 slats from edge closest to you, shiny side down. Dip both hands in finger bowl, shaking off excess. Spread one quarter of rice evenly over nori, leaving a 3/4-inch (2-cm) strip on long side farthest away from you uncovered. Make an indentation across rice about 3/4 inch (2 cm) from side nearest you and put a quarter of carrots, egg and one scallion evenly from one side of rice to the other. Using your index finger and thumb, pick up edge of bamboo mat nearest you. Place remaining fingers over fillings to hold them as you roll mat forward, tightly wrapping rice and nori around fillings. The strip of nori without rice should still be visible.

Press firmly and continue rolling forward to complete roll. Gently press mat to shape roll. Unroll mat and place roll on cutting board with seam on bottom.

Wipe a knife with a damp cloth and cut roll into 8 pieces, wiping knife with each cut. Repeat with remaining rolls. Serve with Japanese soy sauce.

Makes 4 rolls (32 pieces)

Variation

Use a mixture of cooked brown and white rice for added flavor, texture and visual appeal.

PICKLED PLUM AND BROWN RICE SUSHI ROLLS

sushi molds

Bite-sized sushi

3 cups (15 oz/450 g) Sushi rice (see page 28)

2 tablespoons white sesame seeds, toasted

$^1/_2$ cup Seasoned shiitake mushrooms (see page 24)

4 Seasoned kampyo (see page 24)

4 scallions (shallots/spring onions), green parts
   only, blanched

1 Thin seasoned omelette (see page 26), cut into
   $^1/_2$-inch (1-cm) strips

$^1/_2$ red bell pepper (capsicum), seeded and
   thinly sliced

1 English (hothouse) cucumber, seeded and thinly
   sliced lengthwise

1 sheet nori

$^1/_3$ cup (3 fl oz/90 ml) Japanese soy sauce

finger bowl: water with a splash of rice vinegar

Hints

*Look for molds especially designed for sushi or
Japanese rice balls. Cheap alternatives are: cookie
or scone cutters, ice cream scoops, ice cube trays,
mini cup-cake molds, small cups and jelly molds.
Keep in mind that sushi should be bite-sized so use
small molds or cut large sushi before serving.*

In a large bowl, combine sushi rice, sesame seeds and shiitake. Line a sushi mold or loaf cake tin, 8 inches by 3½ inches (20 cm by 9 cm) with plastic wrap, allowing excess to fold over the sides. Arrange alternate strips of kampyo, scallion, omelette, bell pepper and cucumber decoratively as the base. Dip both hands in finger bowl, shaking off excess. Spread a thin layer of sushi rice over vegetables, being careful not to disturb vegetable arrangement. Fold nori sheet in half, not parallel with lines marked on rough side. Lay one half sheet of nori on top of rice. Cover nori completely with another thin layer of rice. Press down gently with fingers or back of a spoon. Lay other half sheet of nori on rice. Set a plate on mold, making sure plastic is not under nori. Hold plate and mold firmly and turn over. Remove mold. Leave sushi wrapped in plastic until ready to serve. Wipe a sharp knife with a damp cloth and cut sushi into bite-sized square, rectangular or diamond shaped pieces. Peel off plastic and serve with soy sauce.

Makes 1 bar (about 16 pieces)

Seasoned carrot sushi

(Nigiri-zushi)

1 cup (5 oz/150 g) Sushi rice (see page 28)

1 large Seasoned carrot (see page 24), thinly
   sliced diagonally

10 scallions (shallots/spring onions), green parts
   only, blanched

1 teaspoon peeled and grated fresh ginger

Teriyaki sauce (see page 105), for
   dipping (optional)

finger bowl: water with a splash of rice vinegar

Shape rice into 10 balls. Pick up a seasoned carrot slice with one hand, bending your fingers to form a shallow mold that carrot can rest in. Place shaped rice rectangle on carrot and very gently press down with index and middle fingers, holding your thumb at top end of rectangle to stop rice being pushed out the end. Turn rice so carrot is on top and continue pushing topping against rice with your index and middle fingers. Turn sushi 180 degrees and repeat. The topping should look like a roof over rice, with very little, if any, rice visible.

Tie a scallion around each sushi and garnish with grated ginger. Serve with Teriyaki sauce for dipping.

Makes 10

SEASONED CARROT SUSHI (NIGIRI-ZUSHI)

Grilled shiitake sushi

(Nigiri-zushi)

1 tablespoon Japanese soy sauce

1 tablespoon mirin

10 fresh shiitake mushrooms, stems removed

1 cup (5 oz/150 g) Sushi rice (see page 28)

1/2 nori sheet sliced into 10 strips, 1/2 inch by 3
    inches (1 cm by 7.5 cm)

finger bowl: water with a splash of rice vinegar

Combine soy sauce and mirin and brush on shiitake. Grill mushrooms until tender, 2–3 minutes. Dip both hands in finger bowl and shake off excess. With one hand, pick up one tablespoon of rice and gently squeeze and shape it into a rectangle with rounded edges. Pick up a mushroom with the other hand, bending your fingers to form a shallow mold that mushroom can rest in. Place shaped rice ball on mushroom and very gently press down with index and middle fingers, holding your thumb at top end of ball to stop rice being pushed out the end.

Turn over rice ball so mushroom is on top and continue gently pushing topping against rice with your index and middle fingers. Turn sushi 180 degrees and repeat. The topping should look like a roof over rice ball, with very little, if any, rice visible. Place a nori strip on top of mushroom and tuck each end underneath rice ball to keep the mushroom in place.

Makes 10

Filling variations

1. *Substitute mushrooms with tofu.*

2. *Seasoned omelette slice tied with blanched scallion, or sliced avocado with wasabi mayonnaise and toasted sesame seeds.*

3. *Pickled radish (takuan) and shiso leaf, tied with Seasoned kampyo strip.*

Seafood options: Sashimi fish (salmon, tuna, kingfish, trevally), squid, cuttlefish and shrimp.

GRILLED SHIITAKE SUSHI (NIGIRI-ZUSHI)

seasoned tofu

Step-by-step
seasoned tofu pouches

(Inari-zushi)

4 large pieces thin deep-fried tofu (abura-age),
  3¹/₄ inches by 5 inches (8 cm by 12.5 cm)

1 cup (8 fl oz/250 ml) Dashi 1 (see page 101)
  or stock

2 tablespoons sugar

2 teaspoons sake

2 tablespoons Japanese soy sauce

Put tofu in a saucepan of boiling water and boil to remove excess oil, about 2 minutes. Drain, gently squeezing out excess water.

In a saucepan, combine tofu, dashi, sugar, sake and soy sauce.

Poke a few holes in a sheet of foil and shape it to fit it inside saucepan so it rests on top of liquid. This drop-lid allows steam to escape but keeps tofu submerged while cooking. Bring to a boil, reduce heat and simmer for 15 minutes. Remove from heat and cool in liquid.

Drain, squeezing out excess liquid. Gently roll over each piece of tofu with a rolling pin to loosen the center.

Cut each piece in half. Gently ease open cut end of each piece with your fingers, pushing down to each corner to form a pouch. These pouches are now ready to be filled with sushi rice.

Tips

Look for ready-made seasoned tofu pouches and seasoned kampyo in packets and cans at Asian grocery stores. Seasoned pouches can be prepared early and refrigerated until required but should be used within 2 to 3 days or frozen for up to 3 months.

Seasoned tofu roll

6 Seasoned tofu pouches (see page 64), 3¹/₄ inches
  by 5 inches (8 cm by 12.5 cm)

1¹/₂ cups (7 oz/225 g) Sushi rice (see page 28)

6 strips pickled radish (takuan) ¹/₂ inch (1 cm)
  thick and 3¹/₄ inches (8 cm) long

6 strips Seasoned kampyo (see page 24) about
  3¹/₄ inch (8 cm)

1 tablespoon toasted sesame seeds (see page 23)

18 scallions (shallots/spring onions), green parts
  only, blanched then well drained

finger bowl: water with a splash of rice vinegar

Cut open two short sides of seasoned tofu pouches and open out flat, short side towards you, rough side up. Dip both hands in finger bowl, shaking off excess. Spread one sixth of rice on each tofu sheet, leaving a ½-inch (1-cm) strip at the front and a ¾-inch (2-cm) strip on side farthest away uncovered. Lay 1 strip radish and kampyo across center of rice and sprinkle with sesame seeds. Pick up edge of tofu and roll up tightly. Tie 3 scallions around each roll about ¾ inch (2 cm) apart. Cut between each tie. Serve some pieces facing up and some on their side for variation.

Makes 6 rolls (18 pieces)

Pickled ginger tofu roll

1 tablespoon finely chopped beni-shoga or gari

2 scallions (shallots/spring onions), green parts
  only, finely sliced

1¹/₂ cups (7 oz/225 g) Sushi rice (see page 28)

6 Seasoned tofu pouches (see page 64), 3¹/₄ inches
  by 2¹/₂ inches (8 cm by 6.5 cm)

finger bowl: water with a splash of rice vinegar

Fold beni-shoga and scallions through rice. Cut open two short sides of tofu pouches and open out flat, short side towards you, rough side up. Dip both hands into finger bowl, shaking off excess. Spread one sixth of rice mixture on each tofu sheet, leaving a ½-inch (12-mm) strip at front end and a ¾-inch (2-cm) strip on farthest side uncovered. Pick up edge of tofu and roll up tightly. Cut each roll in half or thirds.

Makes 6 rolls (12–18 pieces)

SEASONED TOFU ROLL

Somen noodle sushi

4 cups (32 fl oz/1 L) water

3 oz (90 g) dried thin somen noodles

2 sheets nori

1 small carrot, thinly sliced

3 scallions (shallots/spring onions), thinly sliced

1 small red bell pepper (capsicum), thinly sliced

1 tablespoon finely chopped fresh cilantro
   (coriander) leaves

finger bowl: water with a splash of rice vinegar

FOR DIPPING SAUCE

$1/_4$ cup (2 fl oz/60 ml) rice vinegar

2 tablespoons Japanese soy sauce

$1/_4$ teaspoon finely chopped chili pepper

$1/_4$ teaspoon ground (minced) garlic

1 teaspoon sugar

lime or lemon juice, to taste

In a large saucepan over high heat, bring water to a boil. Add noodles and cook until tender, about 3 minutes. Drain and rinse under cold water. Drain and pat dry with paper towel.

Cut nori in half parallel with lines marked on rough side. Place one nori sheet lengthwise on bamboo mat, 3 slats from edge closest to you, shiny side down. Place one quarter of noodles on nori along long side nearest you. Add one quarter of carrot slices, scallions, bell pepper and cilantro. Using your index finger and thumb, pick up bamboo mat and, holding fillings in place with other fingers, roll nori over fillings tightly. Unroll mat and place roll on cutting board with seam on bottom. Wipe a sharp knife with a damp cloth and cut roll into 6 pieces, wiping knife with each cut. Repeat with remaining rolls. Serve with dipping sauce.

To make dipping sauce: In a small bowl, combine ingredients, stirring until sugar dissolves.

Makes 4 rolls (24 pieces)

Variation

Substitute nori with 4–8 savoy cabbage leaves, blanched in hot water to soften, hard stems removed.

SOMEN NOODLE SUSHI

Soba noodle sushi

8 cups (64 fl oz/2 L) water

6 oz (180 g) dried soba noodles

2 tablespoons finely sliced scallions
(shallots/spring onions), green part only

1½ tablespoons light soy sauce

1½ tablespoons rice vinegar

1 tablespoon vegetable oil

1 teaspoon wasabi

2 tablespoons finely chopped gari or beni-shoga

4 sheets nori

1 English (hothouse) cucumber, seeded and finely
sliced lengthwise, skin on

1 red bell pepper (capsicum), seeded and
thinly sliced

1 carrot, thinly sliced lengthwise or grated

1 tablespoon toasted white sesame seeds

¼ cup (2 fl oz/60 ml) Japanese soy sauce

finger bowl: water with a splash of rice vinegar

In a large pot over high heat, bring water to a boil. Gradually add noodles so they do not stick together. Return water to a boil then reduce heat and simmer until noodles are tender but still al dente, 8–10 minutes. Drain and rinse under cold water. Drain again and pat dry with paper towel. Combine noodles, scallions, soy sauce, vinegar, oil, wasabi and gari, adjusting seasoning to taste.

Place one nori sheet lengthwise on a bamboo mat, about 3 slats from edge nearest you, shiny side down. Dip both hands in finger bowl, shaking off excess. Lay a quarter of noodle mixture across bottom third of nori, making sure it extends completely to each end. Add a quarter of cucumber, bell pepper and carrot strips. Using your index finger and thumb, pick up bamboo mat and, holding fillings in place with remaining fingers, roll nori over noodles. Unroll mat and place roll on cutting board with seam on bottom. Repeat for remaining rolls. Wipe a sharp knife with a damp cloth and cut roll into 8 pieces, wiping knife with each cut. Repeat for remaining rolls. Sprinkle with toasted sesame seeds and serve with soy sauce and extra gari and wasabi (if desired).

Makes 4 rolls (32 pieces)

SOBA NOODLE SUSHI

Cellophane sushi

4 oz (125 g) dried cellophane noodles

2 teaspoons rice vinegar

1 teaspoon sugar

pinch salt

2 scallions (shallots/spring onions), green parts
only, thinly sliced

4 sheets nori

2 teaspoons wasabi paste

1/2 English (hothouse) cucumber, seeded and thinly
sliced, skin on

1/2 red bell pepper (capsicum), thinly sliced

1 small carrot, peeled, thinly sliced lengthwise

1 cup (2 oz/60 g) snow pea (mange-tout) sprouts

1/4 cup (2 fl oz/60 ml) Miso sesame dipping sauce,
Ginger sesame, or Chili soy sauce, for dipping
(see page 104)

finger bowl: water with a splash of rice vinegar

Put noodles in a large bowl, cover with boiling water and soak until tender, 3–5 minutes. Rinse under cold water, drain well and pat dry with paper towel. Combine vinegar, sugar and salt, stirring until sugar dissolves. Mix with noodles and scallions.

Place one nori sheet lengthwise on bamboo mat about 3 slats from edge nearest you, shiny side down. Dip both hands in finger bowl, shaking off excess. Spread a quarter of noodles evenly over nori, leaving a 1½-inch (4-cm) strip on farthest side uncovered. Make a hollow across center of noodles. Spread a pinch of wasabi across noodles and top with strips of cucumber, bell pepper, carrot and snow pea sprouts. Using your index finger and thumb, pick up bamboo mat, holding fillings in place with other fingers, roll nori over noodles. Unroll mat and place roll on cutting board with seam on bottom. Wipe a sharp knife with a damp cloth and cut roll into 6 or 8 pieces, wiping knife with each cut. Repeat for remaining rolls. Serve with choice of dipping sauces.

Makes 4 rolls (32 pieces)

Variations

Grill the bell pepper or substitute roasted or antipasto vegetables such as eggplant (aubergine) and zucchini.

CELLOPHANE SUSHI

Battleship sushi

1 teaspoon wasabi paste

2 tablespoons mayonnaise

$^1/_2$ small avocado, finely diced

1 scallion (shallot/spring onion), green part only,
   finely sliced

1 cup (5 oz/150 g) Sushi rice (see page 28)

1 sheet nori, cut into 1-inch by 5-inch
   (2.5-cm by 13-cm) strips

1 teaspoon toasted black sesame seeds

$^1/_4$ small English (hothouse) cucumber, seeded and
   finely sliced, skin on

$^1/_4$ cup (2 fl oz/60 ml) Japanese soy sauce

2 teaspoons beni-shoga

finger bowl: water with a splash of rice vinegar

Mix wasabi and mayonnaise until smooth. Carefully fold in avocado and scallion. Dip both hands in finger bowl, shaking off excess. Gently shape about one tablespoon of rice into a small oval or rectangle. Place one nori strip against rice, shiny side out. Press gently and continue to wrap strip around rice ball. Use a grain of rice to seal overlapped ends of nori.

Cover top of rice with avocado mixture. Sprinkle with sesame seeds. Tuck 3–4 cucumber slices in at one end. Repeat for remaining sushi. Serve with soy sauce and beni-shoga.

Makes 10

Variation

Use 2 teaspoons of rice and smaller nori strips to make mini battleship sushi.

Sushi bars

1 English (hothouse) cucumber

pickled radish (takuan)

2 green shiso leaves

2 strips Seasoned kampyo (see page 24)

1/3 red bell pepper (capsicum), seeded

1/4 teaspoon salt

3 cups (15 oz/450 g) Sushi rice (see page 28)

1 tablespoon toasted white sesame seeds

1–2 teaspoons wasabi paste

1–2 tablespoons gari

1/4 cup (2 fl oz/60 ml) Japanese soy sauce

finger bowl: water with a splash of rice vinegar

Cut cucumber in half and thinly slice, lengthwise. Sprinkle with salt and let stand until soft and pliable. Cut cucumber, radish, shiso, kampyo and bell pepper into strips 2½ inches (7 cm) long. Lay a piece plastic wrap on bamboo mat and alternate half of vegetable strips diagonally across middle, until the arrangement is about 8 inches (20 cm) long. Spread a thin layer of wasabi across the middle. Dip both hands into finger bowl, shaking off excess. Shape half rice into rough bar shape and place on vegetables. Pick up mat with fingers and roll over rice, pressing firmly and gently pulling plastic forward so it is clear of roll. Complete roll with vegetables on top. Allow to set 1–2 minutes. Unroll mat but leave roll in plastic wrap. Wipe a sharp knife with a damp cloth and cut into 8 pieces, wiping knife with each cut. Carefully peel off plastic. Repeat for remaining roll. Serve with gari and soy sauce.

Makes 2 rolls (16 pieces)

Variation

Substitute other thinly sliced vegetables including prepared pickled vegetables which are readily available at Asian markets, such as zucchini, chargrilled eggplant, scallions (green part), seasoned tofu and tempeh.

Seafood options: smoked or sashimi salmon, chives.

Decorative square sushi

4 cups (20 oz/600 g) Sushi rice (see page 28)

food coloring

3 sheets nori

1 strip pickled radish, Thick seasoned omelette
   (see page 26) or cooked carrot, cut ⁵/₈ inch by
   7 inches (1.5 cm by 18 cm) thick

finger bowl: water with a splash of rice vinegar

Divide rice in half and add 1–2 drops of food coloring to one half, leaving half the rice white.

Slightly overlap one full nori sheet and two thirds of a second nori sheet, sealing sheets with a few grains of rice. Dip both hands in finger bowl, shaking off excess. Spread white rice over half the nori and colored rice over the second half, leaving a ¾-inch (2-cm) strip on side farthest from you uncovered. Pick up edge of nori nearest you and roll tightly to the end. Wipe a sharp knife with a damp cloth and cut roll lengthwise into quarters, pressing knife forward so roll does not break apart.

Slightly overlap one full nori sheet with remaining one third nori sheet, sealing with a few grains of rice. Place on bamboo mat. Arrange cut rolls along edge closest to you so they form a square, cut sides outward, with radish strip in center. Pick up edge of the mat nearest you, roll forward, shaping gently with mat to form a square roll. Unroll mat and place roll on cutting board, seam on bottom. Wipe a sharp knife with a damp cloth and cut roll into 8 pieces, wiping knife with each cut.

Makes 8 pieces

Variation

Use half sheets of nori to make small square rolls.

DECORATIVE SQUARE SUSHI

Camellia sushi

1 Thin seasoned omelette (see page 26), cut in
   2-inch (5-cm) squares

4 shiso leaves or 4 pieces nori, cut into 1½-inches
   (4-cm) squares

2 teaspoons wasabi paste

2 cups (10 oz/300 g) Sushi rice (see page 28)

2 teaspoons finely chopped pickled
   radish (takuan)

2 teaspoons finely chopped gari or beni-shoga

1 scallion (shallot/spring onion), green part only,
   finely sliced

¼ cup (2 fl oz/60 ml) Japanese soy sauce

pesticide free camellia or lemon leaves cut into
   edible flower shapes, for serving

finger bowl: water with a splash of rice vinegar

Dip both hands into finger bowl, shaking off excess. Place a slice of omelette and shiso leaf in center of a cloth or plastic wrap. Spread a dab of wasabi in middle. Gently shape about 2 tablespoons of rice into a small ball and set on top of wasabi. Gently twist cloth or plastic and with your finger and, through cloth, make a small indent in center of each ball. Unwrap carefully and place on a plate. Fill indent with finely chopped radish, gari or scallion. Repeat for remaining balls. On a platter, arrange camellia or lemon leaves around sushi and serve with soy sauce.

Makes 10–12 pieces

Variations

Seafood options: Thin slices smoked or sashimi salmon or tuna with salmon roe or flying fish roe or finely chopped egg yolk in the center.

CAMELLIA SUSHI

Wisteria sushi

6 snow peas (mange-tout), trimmed

2 cups (10 oz/300 g) Sushi rice (see page 28)

$^1/_4$ cup (1 oz/30 g) finely diced pickled

   radish (takuan)

2 sheets nori

1–2 teaspoons wasabi paste

2 tablespoons gari

$^1/_4$ cup (2 fl oz/60 ml) Japanese soy sauce

finger bowl: water with a splash of rice vinegar

These rice rolls are a delicious solution for nori cut the wrong way. across lines marked on rough side of sheet. as opposed to parallel to lines. These nori sheets will be longer. but not as wide so you will have less to wrap around rice and fillings. These sheets can be used to make sushi rolls but with less rice. smaller fillings or to make wisteria rolls.

In a saucepan, gently boil snow peas until just cooked but still crisp, 1–2 minutes. Rinse under cold running water to prevent over-cooking and set color. Finely chop. Stir chopped snow peas through half the rice and radish through remaining rice. Cut each nori sheet in half across lines marked on rough side. Lay one half nori sheet lengthwise on bamboo mat, about 3 slats from edge, shiny side down.

Dip both hands in finger bowl, shaking off excess. Spread one half of one rice in center of nori, leaving a ½-inch (1-cm) strip of nori on long side farthest away uncovered. Pick up edge of mat nearest you and roll forward so rice on one side touches rice on far side. Unroll mat. Gently press edges together to form a teardrop-shaped roll, tucking small nori strip around end. Repeat for remaining rolls.

Place 4 rolls next to each other on a cutting board. Wipe a sharp knife with a damp cloth and cut all rolls in half. Cut each half into 4 pieces, wiping knife between cuts. Turn each row of teardrop sushi pieces up so the rice is displayed on top. Arrange two rows next to each other to resemble a spray of wisteria flowers. Serve with wasabi, gari and Japanese soy sauce.

Makes 4 rolls (32 pieces)

Variations

1. *Try blanched asparagus or seasoned baby carrots as fillings.*

2. *Finely chop gari or beni-shoga, pickles, vegetables or herbs and fold through rice.*

3. *Finely chop omelette, scrambled or hard boiled egg and shiso leaves and fold through rice.*

4. *For contrasting flowers add a few drops of different food colorings to rice.*

Leaf sushi

1–2 English (hothouse) or telegraph cucumber,
 skin on

1½ sheets nori

1 cup (5 oz/150 g) Sushi rice (see page 28)

1 teaspoon wasabi

1 tablespoon gari

¼ cup (2 fl oz/60 ml) Japanese soy sauce

finger bowl: water with a splash of rice vinegar

Trim cucumber to the same length as nori sheet, 7¼ inches (18 cm). (Two cucumbers may be needed if using small cucumbers.) Cut cucumber lengthwise into quarters and remove seeds and half the flesh. Cut large nori sheet in half lengthwise, parallel with lines marked on rough side. Cut one half nori sheet lengthwise into strips the same width as cucumber. Join two pieces of cucumber together with a strip of nori in middle. Place one half nori sheet lengthwise on a bamboo mat, about 3 slats from edge closest to you, shiny side down. Cover with rice, leaving a ½-inch (12-mm) strip on both long sides uncovered. Spread a dab of wasabi and the cucumber across rice ½ inch (12 mm) from edge of rice farthest away, making sure cucumber extends fully from end to end.

Using your index finger and thumb, pick up bamboo mat and, holding cucumber in place with other fingers, roll forward tightly until rice touches rice on opposite side. Tuck nori around and gently shape roll into a tear drop shape. Unroll mat and place roll on cutting board. Wipe a sharp knife with a damp cloth and cut roll into 6 pieces, wiping knife with each cut. Repeat for remaining roll. Serve with gari, soy sauce and remaining wasabi.

Makes 2 rolls (12 pieces)

Variation

Substitute cucumber with strips of pickled radish (takuan) and Seasoned kampyo (see page 24) for nori strips between.

Sushi omelette pouches

6 scallions (shallots/spring onions), green
parts only

6 Thin seasoned omelettes, square or round
(see page 26)

$^1/_3$ cup (2o z/5o g) finely chopped Seasoned
kampyo, (see page 24)

$^1/_3$ cup (2o z/5o g) finely chopped Seasoned
carrots (see page 24)

$^1/_2$ sheet nori, shredded

$1^1/_2$ cups (8 oz/24o g) Sushi rice (see page 28)

2–3 teaspoons beni-shoga (optional)

Trim ends of scallion and dip into boiling water for 30–60 seconds to soften. Rinse under cold water to stop the cooking process and set color. Trim omelettes to 6 inches (15 cm) in diameter. Mix kampyo, carrots and nori into rice and divide into 6 equal portions. Place one portion in center of each omelette piece. Gather up four corners, carefully tying top with a scallion. Alternatively, fold omelette over rice like a package, tucking ends underneath, and tie with scallion. Serve with beni-shoga.

Makes 6 pouches

SUSHI OMELETTE POUCHES

Omelette sushi cones

3 Thin seasoned omelettes (see page 26)

1 cup (5o z/150 g) Sushi rice (see page 28)

1 teaspoon wasabi

1–2 fillings (see list below)

2–3 teaspoons beni-shoga

$^1/_4$ cup (2 fl oz/60 ml) Japanese soy sauce

SUGGESTED FILLINGS

pickled radish (takuan) and Seasoned kampyo (see page 24)

Seasoned carrot (see page 24) and blanched snow peas
   (mange-tout)

pickled radish (takuan) and fresh shiso leaves

cucumber and toasted sesame seeds

Cut each omelette in half. Place about 1½ tablespoons sushi rice in middle. Top with a dab of wasabi and 1–2 fillings. Fold omelette over fillings to form omelette into cone shape. Serve with beni-shoga and soy sauce.

Makes 6 cones

Variations

Seafood options: Sashimi tuna or salmon and shiso leaves; crab meat and cucumber.

Omelette sushi roll

4 Thin seasoned omelettes, square shape (see page 26)

3 cups (15 oz/450 g) Sushi rice (see page 28)

1 teaspoon wasabi

1 English (hothouse) cucumber, seeded and thinly
   sliced lengthwise

$^1/_2$ red bell pepper (capsicum), thinly sliced

1 tablespoon toasted sesame seeds

2–3 tablespoons gari

$^1/_4$ cup (2 fl oz/60 ml) Japanese soy sauce

Cover a bamboo mat with plastic wrap. Lay omelette on plastic and cover with sushi rice, leaving a 1-inch (2.5-cm) strip on long side farthest away uncovered. Spread a thin layer of wasabi across rice and arrange fillings evenly from end to end. Using your index finger and thumb, pick up bamboo mat, and holding fillings in place with other fingers, roll forward tightly, wrapping omelette around fillings. Unroll mat, but leave omelette wrapped in plastic. Place roll on cutting board. Wipe a sharp knife with a damp cloth and cut into 6 pieces, wiping knife with each cut. Serve with gari and soy sauce.

Makes 4 rolls (24 pieces)

OMELETTE SUSHI CONES

sushi in a bowl

Scattered sushi

2 large dried shiitake mushrooms

$^1/_2$ cup (4 fl oz/120 ml) Dashi (see page 101)

2 teaspoons sugar

2 teaspoons mirin

1 small carrot, peeled and julienned

$^1/_2$ cup (1$^1/_2$ oz/45 g) thinly sliced, canned bamboo shoots

2 teaspoons reduced-salt soy sauce

6 thin asparagus spears, blanched

12 snow peas (mange-tout), blanched

1 English (hothouse) cucumber

1 Thin seasoned omelette (see page 26)

5 cups (24 oz/750 g) Sushi rice (see page 28)

2 tablespoons shredded nori strips

$^1/_4$ cup shredded beni-shoga

2 teaspoons wasabi

$^1/_3$ cup (3 fl oz/90 ml) Japanese soy sauce

This bufffet-style sushi is a good party or picnic dish, or family meal. It features a variety of sushi ingredients arranged on a platter or in a lacquerware bento, a Japanese lunch box which can be transported easily, and eaten with chopsticks. Presentation style and ingredients differ from region to region in Japan.

Soak mushrooms in cold water until soft, 20–30 minutes. Discard stems and slice caps thinly. Put dashi, sugar and mirin in a medium saucepan and bring to a boil over moderate heat. Add carrot strips and simmer until cooked but still crisp, about 2 minutes. Using a slotted spoon, remove from liquid and set aside. Add bamboo shoots, mushrooms and soy sauce to liquid and cook about 5 minutes. Remove from heat. Return carrot strips and allow to cool completely. (This preparation can be done ahead.)

Slice asparagus and snow peas diagonally into 1½-inch (4-cm) lengths. Cut cucumber lengthwise into quarters and remove seeds. Thinly slice lengthwise into 2-inch (5-cm) pieces or cut decoratively (see Garnishes page 17). Roll omelette and slice thinly, separating slices with fingertips.

Place rice in lacquered boxes, individual bowls or on one large platter. Arrange a selection of vegetables decoratively on rice and garnish with omelette, nori strips and beni-shoga. Serve with wasabi and soy sauce.

Serves 4

Tofu sushi bowl

FOR MARINADE

¹/₄ teaspoon Asian sesame oil

³/₄-inch (2-cm) piece fresh ginger, peeled
 and grated

1 clove garlic, ground (minced)

1 teaspoon brown sugar

2 tablespoons Japanese soy sauce

¹/₂ cup (4 fl oz/125 ml) sake

pinch salt

10 oz (300 g) firm tofu, drained and sliced into
 pieces ³/₈ inch (1 cm) thick

6 cups (30 oz/900 g) Sushi rice (see page 28)

2 teaspoons toasted white sesame seeds

2–3 tablespoons gari

2 scallions (shallots/spring onions), green parts
 only, thinly sliced

¹/₂ nori sheet, cut into small squares

1–2 teaspoons wasabi paste

To make marinade: Combine ingredients, stirring until sugar dissolves.

Pour marinade over tofu and refrigerate for 20 minutes. Drain well. In a bowl, combine rice and sesame seeds. Place one quarter of rice in each of 4 deep (donburi-style) bowls. Arrange tofu slices in rosette pattern on top. Lay a few slices of gari across a chopping board, each one slightly overlapping the next. Roll from one end and stand up, folding top out slightly to form a rosebud. Place in center of tofu slices and sprinkle top with scallions and nori squares. Serve with wasabi.

Serves 4

Hint

Use this marinade for blanched green beans, snow peas (mange-tout), spinach, carrots and sweet peppers and add to Tofu donburi (above) or use in various sushi.

Seafood option: Substitute sliced sashimi tuna or salmon for tofu.

TOFU SUSHI BOWL

sushi

Mango, ginger and coconut sushi

2 cups (13 oz/400 g) short grain rice

2$^{1}/_{4}$ cups (10 fl oz/300 ml) water

$^{1}/_{3}$ cup (3 fl oz/90 ml) coconut milk

1 teaspoon sugar

$^{3}/_{4}$ teaspoon lime juice

pinch salt

1 small mango, sliced

10 nori strips, about $^{1}/_{2}$ inch by 3 inches
   (1 cm by 7.5 cm)

Passion fruit yogurt (see below)

$^{1}/_{4}$ teaspoon lime zest or lemon curls
   (see Garnishes page 17)

finger bowl: water with a splash of rice vinegar

FOR PASSION FRUIT YOGURT

1 passion fruit

$^{1}/_{3}$ cup (3 oz/80 ml) yogurt

$^{1}/_{2}$ teaspoon honey, or to taste

The coconut rice here is less rich than the coconut rice designed for the Peach and coconut sushi roll (see page 96). They can be interchanged with satisfaction.

Rinse rice three or four times until water runs clear. Drain for 15 minutes. In a medium saucepan or microwave, bring rice and water to a boil. Reduce heat and simmer, covered, until most liquid is absorbed, 12–15 minutes. Remove from heat and stand, covered, to complete cooking process, 10 minutes longer.

Place hot rice in a large bowl or dish. In a separate bowl, combine coconut milk, sugar, lime juice and salt, stirring until sugar dissolves. Sprinkle milk mixture over rice, cutting through rice with a flat spatula or rice paddle. Fan rice to cool to room temperature, about 5 minutes (this can be done with an electric fan on lowest setting).

Dip both hands in finger bowl, shaking off excess. Gently shape 1$^{1}/_{2}$–2 tablespoons of rice with mixture into a rectangle with rounded edges. Place a slice of mango on top so it looks like a roof over rice ball, with very little, if any, rice being visible. Lay a nori strip on top of fruit and tuck each end underneath rice ball to keep fruit in place. Top each ball with a small amount of passion fruit yogurt. Garnish with lime zest. Alternatively, serve yogurt and lime separately, for guests to add to taste.

To make yogurt: Remove passion fruit pulp and combine with yogurt and honey.

Makes 15–20

MANGO. GINGER AND COCONUT SUSHI

Peach and coconut sushi roll

1 1/2 cups (10 oz/300 g) short grain rice

3/4 cup (6 fl oz/180 ml) water

1 cup (8 fl oz/250 ml) coconut milk

1 tablespoon sugar

2 teaspoons lime juice

pinch salt

1/3 cup finely chopped glace ginger

1 peach cut into slices

1/4 teaspoon Japanese soy sauce

2 sheets nori

finger bowl: water with a splash of rice vinegar

Rinse rice three or four times until water runs clear. Drain for 15 minutes. In a medium saucepan or microwave, bring rice, water and coconut cream to a boil. Reduce heat and simmer, covered until most liquid is absorbed, 12–15 minutes. Remove from heat and stand, covered, to complete cooking process, 10 minutes longer.

Place hot rice in large bowl or dish. In a separate bowl, combine sugar, lime juice and salt, stirring until sugar dissolves. Sprinkle sugar mixture over rice, cutting through rice with a flat spatula or rice paddle. Stir in glace ginger. Fan rice to cool to room temperature, about 5 minutes (this can be done with an electric fan on lowest setting). Sprinkle peach slices with soy sauce and set aside.

Cut nori in half, parallel with lines marked on rough side. Place a half nori sheet lengthwise on a bamboo mat, above 3 slats from edge nearest you, shiny side down. Dip both hands in finger bowl, shaking off excess. Cover nori with rice, leaving a 3/4-inch (2-cm) strip on long side farthest away uncovered. Make a small groove in middle of rice with finger and lay peach slices evenly from end to end.

Using your index finger and thumb, pick up edge of bamboo mat nearest you. Place other fingers over fillings to hold them in place as you roll mat forward tightly wrapping rice and nori around fillings. Press gently and continue rolling forward to complete roll. Gently press mat to shape roll. Unroll mat and place roll on cutting board with seam on bottom. Wipe a sharp knife with a damp cloth and cut roll in half. Pick up one half roll and turn it 180 degrees so both cut ends are at the same side. Make 2 cuts through both rolls together to make 6 bite-size pieces, wiping knife with each cut. Repeat for remaining rolls.

Makes 4 rolls (24 pieces)

PEACH AND COCONUT SUSHI ROLL

Lemon sushi rice

1 1/2 cups (10 oz/300 g) short grain rice

1 3/4 cups (14 fl oz/430 ml) water

1/4 cup (2 fl oz/60 ml) lemon juice

2 teaspoons sugar

pinch salt

2 teaspoons finely chopped lemon zest

4 sheets nori

selection of fruit such as strawberries, kiwi fruit
 and paw paw

finger bowl: water with a splash of rice vinegar

Rinse rice 3 or 4 times until water runs clear. Drain for 15 minutes. In a medium saucepan or microwave, bring rice and water to a boil. Reduce heat and simmer, covered, until most of liquid is absorbed, 12–15 minutes. Remove from heat and stand, covered, to complete the cooking process, 10 minutes longer. Place hot rice in a large flat bowl or dish. In a separate bowl, combine lemon juice, sugar, salt and zest, stirring until sugar dissolves. Pour juice over hot rice, cutting through rice with a flat spatula or rice paddle to break up any lumps and distribute flavor evenly. Fan rice to cool to room temperature, about 5 minutes.

Place a nori sheet lengthwise on a bamboo mat about 3 slats from edge closest to you, shiny side down. Dip both hands in finger bowl, shaking off excess and cover nori with rice, except a 3/4-inch (2-cm) strip on long side opposite.

Using your index finger and thumb, pick up edge of bamboo mat nearest you and roll mat forward tightly. Press gently and continue rolling forward to complete roll. Gently press mat to shape roll. Unroll mat and place roll on cutting board with seam on bottom. Wipe a sharp knife with a damp cloth and cut roll in half. Pick up one half roll and turn it 180 degrees so both cut ends are at the same side. Cut roll into about 1/2-inch (1-cm) pieces, wiping knife with each cut, and arrange fruit decoratively on top. Repeat for remaining rolls.

Makes 4 rolls (56 pieces)

Variations

Substitute orange or lime for lemon. Or, slice nashi (pear) thinly and top with lemon or coconut rice and more fruit.

LEMON SUSHI RICE

soups

Steaming bowls of Japanese soups, with pickles and green tea, turn sushi into a simple but complete meal. There are two basic soups served with Japanese meals. Clear (suimono) is a delicate, crystal clear soup made with an artistic arrangement of ingredients. Miso is a thicker soup made with miso paste. Both are made with dashi, a delicate, slightly fishy stock, also used in many other Japanese dishes.

Dashi is made with bonito, fish that has been smoked and dried for six months so that it looks like a piece of old wood. Traditionally, bonito is shaved into flakes just before use so the flavor is not lost, then simmered in water with a piece of konbu (dried seaweed).

Nowadays home cooks use prepared bonito flakes, sold in packets at Asian markets. The large, coarser flakes are for stock, the smaller, finer flakes are generally used as a garnish. Although there is nothing to compare with the flavor of making fresh stock, for a quick stock choose instant dashi granules, available in Asian markets and some larger supermarkets. Simply heat the granules in water, adjusting the flavor strength to taste.

There are two types of dashi, one for the clear stock (Dashi I), with the left-over ingredients being reused to make the second stock (Dashi II), which is then mixed with miso paste to make miso soup. For a stronger flavored miso soup, use Dashi II and add an extra handful of bonito flakes to the stock. The quantity of konbu and bonito can be varied to suit individual tastes.

If you prefer a completely vegetarian stock, use a double quantity of konbu only. Choose good quality konbu with a flat, wide, thick leaf about 10 inches (25 cm) wide. Avoid thin, wrinkled konbu if at all possible. If the konbu expands greatly and develops soft blisters as it simmers, it is of good quality.

Make whichever basic stock is preferred, then add any combination of ingredients for a variety of interesting and tasty soups. Always cook ingredients for clear soups separately, never in the stock or it becomes cloudy. Pour hot stock over any ingredients requiring cooking, so the soup remains clear. Stock made with vegetables other than konbu can be flavorful, but the soup will not be clear.

Miso pastes can vary enormously in flavor, saltiness and texture. As a general rule, the lighter the miso the sweeter the flavor, the darker the miso the saltier the taste. Some miso is smooth textured, some chunky. Often miso soup is made with a combination of miso pastes, so experiment with types and quantities for some interesting results.

Dashi I (Ichiban-dashi)

¼ oz (10 g) piece dried konbu
(seaweed) 8 inches by 4 inches
(20 cm by 10 cm)

4½ cups (36 fl oz/1.1 L) cold water

2 cups (½ oz/15 g) dried bonito
flakes (katsuo-bushi),
loosely packed

Dashi I is a light stock subtly flavored with konbu and shaved bonito flakes and is used for clear soups.

Gently wipe konbu with a damp cloth. (Never wash konbu as much of the flavor on the surface will be washed away.) Make 2 or 3 incisions along edge of konbu to release flavor during cooking. In a large saucepan over moderate heat, combine konbu and four cups water. Slowly bring to a boil, about 8 minutes, but just before water boils remove konbu to avoid a bitter taste. Reserve konbu for Dashi II. Add remaining water to bring down temperature. Add all bonito flakes and bring water to a boil. Immediately turn off heat and allow flakes to settle to bottom of pan. Strain through a sieve lined with cheesecloth or muslin, reserving flakes for Dashi II. Used flakes and konbu will keep refrigerated for 2 days before flavor is lost.

Instant dashi substitute: 1¼–1½ teaspoons instant dashi granules to to 4 cups (32 fl oz/1 L) warm water (according to taste), stirring until granules dissolve.

Makes 4½ cups (36 fl oz/1.1 L)

Dashi II (Niban-dashi)

konbu and bonito flakes left over
from Dashi I

4½ cups (36 fl oz/1.1 L) cold water

½ cup (⅛ oz/4 g) dried bonito
flakes (katsuo-bushi)

This stock, based on seaweed and bonito fish flakes, is generally milder than Dashi I as it reuses the same ingredients. For a stronger taste, add a handful of fresh bonito flakes.

In a large saucepan, combine konbu and bonito flakes reserved from Dashi I with water. Bring to a boil over moderate heat. Reduce heat and gently simmer 15 minutes. Add extra bonito flakes and immediately remove from heat. Allow flakes to settle to bottom. Strain stock and discard flakes. The konbu can be eaten as is or with some miso paste as an appetizer.

Instant dashi substitute: 1½–2 teaspoons instant dashi granules to 4 cups (32 fl oz/1 L) warm water, stirring until granules dissolve.

Makes 4 cups (32 fl oz/1 L)

Leftover dashi

Refrigerate leftover dashi in a sealed container for up to 3 days or freeze for up to 1 month. Some delicate flavor and aroma is lost in storage. Freeze in measured amounts such as cup measurements or a tablespoon in an ice cube tray. Add cooked rice to leftover dashi for a quick and easy soup.

Suimono: clear soup

Suimono means clear soup. Season clear soup (see the three recipes on this page) with soy sauce, which will color it slightly, plus sake and salt. Although quantities of these can be varied to taste, too much soy sauce makes the soup dark and strong flavored. The flavors should remain delicate and the soup clear. For a lighter color use light soy sauce.

Carrot-tofu clear soup

1 piece carrot 4 inches (10 cm) long, peeled

12 green chives, cut into 4-inch (10-cm) lengths

1½ oz (45 g) firm tofu, drained and diced small

4 cups (32 fl oz/1 L) Dashi I (see page 101)

generous pinch salt

1–2 teaspoons Japanese soy sauce, to taste

1 teaspoon sake

1 teaspoon finely chopped lemon peel, lemon curls or triangle lemon twist (see Garnishes, page 17)

Make small v-shaped cuts at ½-inch (12-mm) intervals around carrot. Then cut carrot into ½-inch (12-mm) slices to make eight flowers. Alternatively, use a biscuit cutter to make flowers. Simmer carrot flowers in boiling water or microwave in a covered container with 1 tablespoon water, until cooked but still crisp, 1–2 minutes. Drain. Loosely tie 4 chives into knots. Divide one knot, two carrot flowers and tofu into four soup bowls.

In a medium saucepan bring stock just to a boil. Stir in salt, soy sauce and sake. Carefully ladle into soup bowls. Garnish with finely chopped lemon peel.

Serves 4

Bean-ginger clear soup

4 cups (32 fl oz/1 L) Dashi I (see page 101)

generous pinch salt

1–2 teaspoons Japanese soy sauce, to taste

⅓ cup (2 oz/60 g) green beans, cut into ¾-inch (2-cm) lengths, blanched

4–8 wheaten gluten bread (fu)

1 teaspoon very fine slivers fresh ginger

Prepare soup following instructions for Carrot-tofu clear soup (above), substituting carrot and tofu with beans and fu, garnished with ginger.

Serves 4

Clear soup with noodles

1 cup (3 oz/90 g) dried, thin somen noodles

4 cups (32 fl oz/1 L) Dashi I (see page 101)

generous pinch salt

1–2 teaspoons Japanese soy sauce, to taste

8 medium fresh shiitake mushrooms, halved

2 scallions (shallots/spring onions), thinly sliced

Bring 4 cups (32 fl oz/1 L) water to a boil in a large saucepan. Add noodles and cook until tender, about 3 minutes. Drain and rinse under cold water.

Prepare soup following instructions for Carrot-tofu clear soup (see page 102), substituting carrot and tofu with noodles mushrooms, and scallions.

Serves 4

Miso soup

There are many different miso pastes available, some smooth textures, some chunky, with varying degrees of flavor and saltiness. Most miso pastes are interchangeable in recipes but quantities may need to be adjusted according to taste. As a general rule the darker the miso the saltier the taste, the lighter the miso the sweeter the taste.

Miso soup can be made with a combination of different miso pastes, so experiment with types and quantities. It is advisable to taste miso soup before adding all the miso paste so the taste and saltiness will suit personal preferences.

Miso soup with wakame and tofu

1/4 cup (1/6 oz/5 g) dried wakame seaweed

4 cups (32 fl oz/1 L) Dashi II (see page 101)

3 1/2 oz (100 g) firm tofu, drained and diced

3 tablespoons red miso paste

2 chopped scallions (shallots/spring onions), green parts only

Cover wakame with cold water and let stand to reconstitute and soften, 10–15 minutes. In a large saucepan, bring stock almost to a boil. In a small bowl dissolve miso with some hot stock, stirring until smooth. Gradually add miso mixture into hot stock pan. Add tofu and wakame to heat through. Remove from heat and pour into soup bowls. Garnish with scallions and serve.

Serves 4

Variations: 1. Enoki, shiitake, shimeji mushrooms or a combination of all three and scallions (shallots/spring onions). 2. Bamboo shoots and wakame seaweed. 3. Cooked potato and wakame seaweed, beans or spinach. 4. Daikon and deep-fried tofu (abura-age).

Daikon-carrot miso soup

1/3 cup (2 oz/60 g) daikon (white radish), peeled and julienned

1 small carrot, peeled and julienned

4 cups (32 fl oz/1 L) Dashi II (see page 101)

3–4 tablespoons white miso paste, to taste

2 scallions (shallots/spring onions), thinly sliced

shichimi togarashi (7 spice mix) optional

In a large saucepan bring daikon, carrot and stock to a boil. Reduce heat and simmer until vegetables are cooked but still crisp, 3–4 minutes. In a small bowl dissolve miso with some hot stock, stirring until smooth. Gradually add miso mixture into hot stock pan. Bring almost to a boil, remove from heat and pour into soup bowls. Garnish with scallions and schichimi togarashi.

Variation: Substitute schichimi togarashi with thinly sliced lemon peel or grated fresh ginger.

Serves 4

Seaweed stock

about 3/4 oz (20 g) dried konbu (seaweed), 10 inches by 10 inches (25 cm by 25 cm)

4 1/2 cups (36 fl oz/1.1 L) cold water

Gently wipe konbu with a damp cloth. (Never wash konbu as the flavor on the surface will be washed away). Make two or three incisions along edge of konbu to release flavor during cooking.

Put in a saucepan with water and slowly bring to a simmer but do not boil, about 20 minutes. For a stronger flavor allow longer simmering time. Alternatively, cover konbu with cold water and stand 3–4 hours for flavors to be released. Remove konbu and use stock to make clear or miso soup.

Variation: Add dried shiitake mushrooms to stock for added flavor.

Makes about 4½ cups (36 fl oz/1.1 L)

sauces

Miso sesame sauce

¹/₄ cup (2 fl oz/60 ml) rice vinegar

2 tablespoons water or Dashi stock
   (see page 101)

1 tablespoon white miso paste

1 tablespoon sesame seed paste
   or tahini

1 tablespoon sugar

1 teaspoon toasted white
   sesame seeds

1 scallion (shallot/spring onion),
   green part only, thinly sliced

In a small bowl, combine rice vinegar, water, miso, sesame seed paste and sugar, stirring well until sugar dissolves. Cover and refrigerate until required. Garnish with sesame seeds and scallion.

This sesame sauce can be made 2–3 days ahead and refrigerated until needed. Add finely chopped chili or wasabi for extra bite.

Makes ¾ cup (6 fl oz/180 ml)

Teriyaki sauce

¹/₄ cup (2 fl oz/60 ml) Japanese
   soy sauce

¹/₄ cup (2 fl oz/60 ml) mirin

2 tablespoons sugar

Use this thick sauce as a topping for nigiri-zushi (see page 60). For extra flavor add ground (minced) fresh ginger and garlic to taste.

In a small saucepan over low heat, combine soy sauce, mirin and sugar. Stir well until sugar dissolves. Continue heating to reduce until thickened. Keep sauce refrigerated. Brush sauce on shiitake, eggplant (aubergine) or other vegetables before grilling or pan-frying and then using as a topping for sushi or in sushi rolls (see page 36).

Makes ½ cup (4 fl oz/125 ml)

Ginger sesame sauce

1–2 teaspoons ginger juice, to taste

¹/₂ cup (4 fl oz/125 ml) Japanese
   soy sauce

¹/₄ cup (2 fl oz/60 ml) mirin

¹/₄ cup (2 fl oz/60 ml) sake

¹/₂ teaspoon Asian sesame oil

To obtain ginger juice: Finely grate fresh ginger and squeeze to extract ginger juice. Alternatively, substitute with grated fresh ginger in recipe but decrease to about ½ teaspoon or to taste.

In a small bowl combine ginger juice, soy sauce, mirin, sake, and sesame oil. Stir well. Refrigerate until needed.

Makes 1 cup (8 fl oz/250 ml)

Marinade for vegetables

1 tablespoon rice vinegar

2 tablespoon vegetable oil

1 teaspoon sesame oil

1 teaspoon Japanese soy sauce

pinch salt

This marinade is ideal for blanched green beans, snow peas (mange-tout), spinach, carrots, sweet peppers and tofu. Use the vegetables in sushi rolls (see page 36) or chirashi-zushi (see page 90).

In a small bowl, combine vinegar, oils, soy sauce and salt.

Chili soy sauce

Japanese soy sauce

shichimi togarashi (7 spice mix)
   or fresh red chili, seeded and
   finely sliced

Combine soy sauce with schichimi togarashi or fresh chili, to taste.

pickles

In Japanese cuisine, pickles play many roles. They serve as a filling in sushi, a garnish and a side dish to many dishes. Pickles enhance the flavor of other foods, cleanse the palate and aid digestion. There are many pickled vegetables available from Asian grocery stores, and all will keep well if stored in an airtight container and refrigerated.

Some of the most popular prepared pickles are beni-shoga (pickled ginger slices) and gari (pink pickled ginger). Both are available in packets, either sliced or shredded. The pink is slightly sweeter, the red slightly saltier. Pink is traditionally used as a garnish for sushi and sashimi.

Another popular prepared item is pickled daikon (long white radish), also known as takuan. Thinly sliced in a small dish, it is served with meals to cleanse the palate. Sliced lengthwise, it is used as a filling in sushi rolls. Kimchee, Korean pickled cabbage, is also readily available and sometimes served with sushi.

It is easy to make your own pickles from Chinese cabbage, cucumber (peeled and seeded if not a hothouse or telegraph cucumber), eggplant (aubergine), carrot or cauliflower.

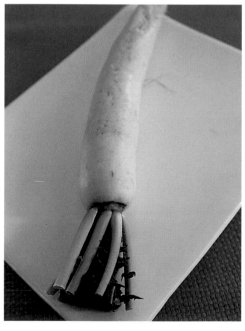

DAIKON

GINGER

CUCUMBER

Pickled carrot and daikon

1 medium carrot

3-inch (7.5-cm) piece daikon

1 teaspoon salt

3 tablespoons rice vinegar

1/2 teaspoon Japanese soy sauce

1/8 teaspoon peeled and grated
   fresh ginger

2 teaspoons sugar

Peel and finely shred carrot and daikon. Put into large bowl, sprinkle with salt and let stand for 30 minutes. Gently squeeze out as much water as possible from vegetables. In a bowl, combine vinegar, soy sauce, ginger and sugar, stirring until sugar dissolves. Add vegetables and refrigerate for 8 hours. Pickled carrot and daikon will keep for one week if refrigerated in an airtight container.

Quick variation: Soak shredded carrot and daikon separately for 15 minutes in cold water. Drain well and sprinkle with sushi vinegar before serving.

Pickled ginger

3-4 pieces fresh ginger, peeled and
   thinly sliced along the grain

salt

1/2 cup (4 fl oz/125 ml) rice vinegar

2 tablespoons sugar, or to taste

1/4 cup (2 fl oz/60 ml) water

Pickled ginger will keep for several months if refrigerated in an airtight container. Allow 1–2 tablespoons per person for a sushi meal. Eat with fingers or chopsticks.

Spread ginger slices in a colander and sprinkle with salt. Let stand until soft, 30 minutes or longer. Drop ginger into boiling water to blanch. Drain and cool.

In a bowl, combine rice vinegar, sugar and water, stirring well until sugar dissolves. Add ginger and refrigerate until well seasoned, about one day. The ginger will turn pinkish in the marinade. For more color add a drop of pink food coloring to the marinade.

Pickled cucumber

1 English (hothouse) cucumber,
   thinly sliced

2 teaspoons salt

1/4 cup (2 fl oz/60 ml) Sushi vinegar
   (see page 28)

Put cucumbers in a bowl, sprinkle with salt and let stand for 5 minutes. Rinse under cold water to remove salt. Sprinkle with sushi vinegar and refrigerate overnight. Serve in a small bowl. If a milder vinegar flavor is preferred, heat the vinegar for 1 minute.

Index

Guide to weights and measures

The conversions given in the recipes in this book are approximate. Whichever system you use, remember to follow it consistently, thereby ensuring that the proportions are consistent throughout a recipe.

WEIGHTS

Imperial	Metric
1/3 oz	10 g
1/2 oz	15 g
3/4 oz	20 g
1 oz	30 g
2 oz	60 g
3 oz	90 g
4 oz (1/4 lb)	125 g
5 oz (1/3 lb)	150 g
6 oz	180 g
7 oz	220 g
8 oz (1/2 lb)	250 g
9 oz	280 g
10 oz	300 g
11 oz	330 g
12 oz (3/4 lb)	375 g
16 oz (1 lb)	500 g
2 lb	1 kg
3 lb	1.5 kg
4 lb	2 kg

USEFUL CONVERSIONS

1/4 teaspoon	1.25 ml
1/2 teaspoon	2.5 ml
1 teaspoon	5 ml
1 Australian tablespoon	20 ml (4 teaspoons)
1 UK/US tablespoon	15 ml (3 teaspoons)

Butter/Shortening

1 tablespoon	1/2 oz	15 g
1 1/2 tablespoons	3/4 oz	20 g
2 tablespoons	1 oz	30 g
3 tablespoons	1 1/2 oz	45 g

OVEN TEMPERATURE GUIDE

The Celsius (°C) and Fahrenheit (°F) temperatures in this chart apply to most electric ovens. Decrease by 25°F or 10°C for a gas oven or refer to the manufacturer's temperature guide. For temperatures below 325°F (160°C), do not decrease the given temperature.

VOLUME

Imperial	Metric	Cup
1 fl oz	30 ml	
2 fl oz	60 ml	1/4
3 fl oz	90 ml	1/3
4 fl oz	125 ml	1/2
5 fl oz	150 ml	2/3
6 fl oz	180 ml	3/4
8 fl oz	250 ml	1
10 fl oz	300 ml	1 1/4
12 fl oz	375 ml	1 1/2
13 fl oz	400 ml	1 2/3
14 fl oz	440 ml	1 3/4
16 fl oz	500 ml	2
24 fl oz	750 ml	3
32 fl oz	1L	4

Oven description	°C	°F	Gas Mark
Cool	110	225	1/4
	130	250	1/2
Very slow	140	275	1
	150	300	2
Slow	170	325	3
Moderate	180	350	4
	190	375	5
Moderately Hot	200	400	6
Fairly Hot	220	425	7
Hot	230	450	8
Very Hot	240	475	9
Extremely Hot	250	500	10

First published in the United States in 2001 by Periplus Editions (HK) Ltd.,
with editorial offices at 364 Innovation Drive, North Clarendon, Vermont 05759 and
130 Joo Seng Road, #06-01/03, Singapore 368357

LCC Card No. 2003277653
ISBN-13: 978-0-7946-5002-5
ISBN-10: 0-7946-5002-3

DISTRIBUTED BY

North America, Latin America & Europe
(*English Language*)
Tuttle Publishing
364 Innovation Drive
North Clarendon, VT 05759-9436
Tel: (802) 773-8930 Fax: (802) 773-6993
Email: info@tuttlepublishing.com
www.tuttlepublishing.com

Japan
Tuttle Publishing
Yaekari Building, 3rd Floor
5-4-12 Osaki, Shinagawa-ku
Tokyo 141-0032
Tel: (03) 5437-0171 Fax: (03) 5437-0755
Email: tuttle-sales@gol.com

Asia Pacific
Berkeley Books Pte Ltd
130 Joo Seng Road #06-01/03
Singapore 368357
Tel: (65) 6280 1330 Fax: (65) 6280 6290
Email: inquiries@periplus.com.sg
www.periplus.com

Set in Frutiger on QuarkXpress
Printed in Singapore

First Edition

06 07 08 09 10   8 7 6 5 4 3